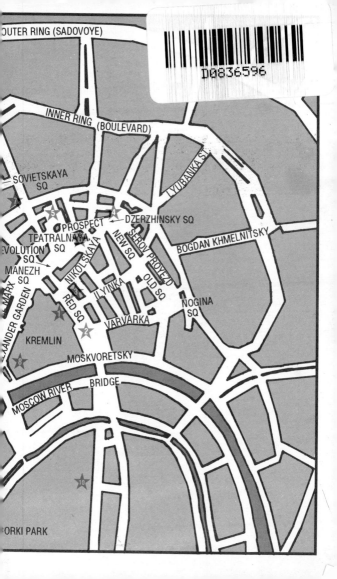

RUSSIAN
AT A GLANCE

PHRASE BOOK & DICTIONARY FOR TRAVELERS

BY THOMAS R. BEYER, JR.
C.V. Starr Professor of Russian
Dean, The Russian School
Middlebury College
Middlebury, Vermont

BARRON'S

BARRON'S EDUCATIONAL SERIES, INC.

Cover and Book Design   Milton Glaser, Inc.
Illustrations   Juan Suarez
Typesetting   Friedrich Typography, Santa Barbara

All inquiries should be addressed to:
Barron's Educational Series, Inc.
250 Wireless Boulevard
Hauppauge, New York 11788

Library of Congress Catalog Card Number 90-24237

Paper Edition
International Standard Book No. 0-8120-4299-9

Library of Congress Cataloging-in-Publication Data

Beyer, Thomas R.
  Russian at a glance: phrase book and dictionary for travelers/
by Thomas R. Beyer, Jr.
      p.   cm.
  Includes index.
  ISBN 0-8120-4299-9
  1. Russian language—Conversation and phrase books—English.
I. Title.
PG2121.B49   1991
491.783'421—dc20   90-24237
                                                          CIP

PRINTED IN THE UNITED STATES OF AMERICA

34   9770   9876

CONTENTS

PREFACE

So you're taking a trip to one of the most fascinating countries in the world. That's exciting! In more ways than one, this new phrase book will prove an invaluable companion that will make your stay far more interesting and truly unforgettable.

This phrase book is part of a series published by Barron's Educational Series, Inc. In these books we present the phrases and words that a traveler most often needs for a brief visit to a foreign country, where the customs and language are often different. Each of these phrase books highlights the terms particular to that country, in situations that the tourist is most likely to encounter. With a specially developed key to pronunciation, this book will enable you to communicate quickly and confidently in colloquial terms. It is intended not only for beginners with no knowledge of the language, but also for those who have studied Russian and have some familiarity with it.

Some of the unique features and highlights of the Barron's series are:

■ Easy to follow *pronunciation keys* and complete phonetic transcriptions of all words and phrases in the book.

■ Compact dictionary of commonly used words and phrases—built right into the phrase book so there's no need to carry a separate dictionary.

■ Useful phrases for the *tourist*, grouped together by subject matter in a logical way so that the appropriate phrase is easy to locate when you need it.

■ Special phrases for the *business traveler*, including banking terms.

■ Comprehensive section on *food and drink*, with food terms you will find on menus; these terms are often difficult or impossible to locate in dictionaries.

■ *Emergency phrases* and terms we hope you won't need: medical problems, theft or loss of valuables, replacement or repair of watches, cameras, and the like.

■ *Sightseeing itineraries*, shopping tips, practical travel tips to help you get off the beaten path and into the countryside, to the small towns and cities, and to neighboring areas.

■ A *reference section* providing: important signs, conversion tables, holidays, time phrases, days of the week, and months of the year.

■ A brief *grammar section,* with the basic elements of the language briefly explained.

Enjoy your vacation and travel with confidence. You have a friend by your side.

ACKNOWLEDGMENTS

I would like to thank the following individuals and organizations for their assistance on this project:

Elena Kochneva of the Pushkin Russian Language Institute, Aeroflot, and Intourist. Mostly I am grateful to the dozens of friendly and courteous Russians in Moscow and Leningrad, including the "key ladies," my shoe shine man, the hairdressers at the Leningrad Hotel, the attendants at the Krasnopresnensky Baths, the lovely woman at the watch repair shop on Pushkin Street, the taxi drivers, and all who ensured that words and phrases in the book reflect the current state of the Russian language.

INTRODUCTION TO THE RUSSIAN LANGUAGE

Russian today is still spoken by the overwhelming majority of people in the former Soviet Union. It is the native language of approximately half of the population. But the Soviet Union was a multinational society, with over two hundred languages and dialects. Thus, many of the individuals whom you encounter will speak and understand Russian as a second language. It is important that you recognize and respect the difference between Russia and the newly independent states created out of the former republics of the Soviet Union. People will appreciate your awareness that not everyone in their country is Russian. Especially when traveling to the other countries, I have found it useful to learn a few courtesy phrases, such as *Hello, Thank you, Please*, and *You're welcome* in the local language.

Russian is a Slavic language, closest to Ukrainian and White Russian, but also related to Polish, Czech, Slovak, Slovenian, Croatian, Serbian, Macedonian, and Bulgarian. Its alphabet dates to the ninth century, when the monks Cyril and Methodius developed a written language for the Slavs. The Cyrillic alphabet, as it is called, has much in common with the Greek alphabet. With a little work you will be able to read the signs and texts that make most of Russia still a mystery for many Westerners. Most Russians are delighted and flattered by foreigners who attempt to speak their language. Your efforts will be generously rewarded.

TRAVEL TIP

Your longest wait in Russia may be for your suitcases to come off the plane. You can save yourself considerable time and irritation by packing any belongings in a carry-on bag. If you travel light you can easily fit in a week's clothing and personal goods. Remember that bags must be able to fit under the airplane seat, even though many major airlines now have spacious overhead bins. If in doubt, check with the airline concerning the dimensions for carry-ons.

QUICK PRONUNCIATION GUIDE

The Cyrillic alphabet has thirty-three letters. Many of them will be familiar to you from English, and several others resemble Greek letters. As in English, each letter is only an approximation of how a sound is pronounced. The guide below should get you started in speaking Russian.

STRESS

Each Russian word has only one syllable that is stressed or under accent. Russians know where the stress is and do not write the accent marks. We will indicate the stressed syllable with capital letters in our transcription as an aid for your pronunciation.

VOWELS

Russian has five vowel sounds, but ten vowel letters. Five of the letters are "hard" and five are "soft." The one vowel sound in each word which is stressed receives special emphasis. As you speak Russian try, in the beginning, to exaggerate your pronunciation.

RUSSIAN LETTER	RUSSIAN SOUND	ENGLISH SYMBOL	EXAMPLE	
HARD VOWELS				
а	a as in Amen	*A**	да	*DA*
э	e as in echo	*E*	эхо	*Ekho*
ы	y as in hairy	*Y*	мы	*MY*
о	o as in hello	*O*	но	*NO*
у	u as in rule	*U*	ну	*NU*

*Any English symbol may appear either capitalized (*A*) indicating that it is stressed, or lower case (*a*) indicating that it is not stressed.

RUSSIAN LETTER	RUSSIAN SOUND	ENGLISH SYMBOL	EXAMPLE

SOFT VOWELS

я	ya as in yahoo	YA	я *YA*
е	ye as in yes	YE	нет *NYET*
и	ee as in bee	I	ива *Iva*
ё	yo as in yo-yo	YO	полёт *paLYOT*
ю	u as in union	YU	юмор *YUmar*

CONSONANT LETTERS

б	b as in bat	B	банк *BANK*
в	v as in vote	V	вот *VOT*
г	g as in go	G	гол *GOL*
д	d as in dog	D	да *DA*
ж	zh as in azure	ZH	жена *zhiNA*
з	z as in zoo	Z	за *ZA*
й	y as in boy	Y	мой *MOY*
к	k as in kayak	K	касса *KAsa*
л	l as in lot	L	лампа *LAMpa*
м	m as in mall	M	муж *MUSH*
н	n as in note	N	нос *NOS*
п	p as in papa	P	парк *PARK*
р	r as in rabbit	R	рот *ROT*
с	s as in sun	S	суп *SUP*
т	t as in toe	T	такси *taKSI*
ф	f as in fund	F	фунт *FUNT*
х	ch as in Bach, loch	KH	ах *AKH*
ц	ts as in tsar	TS	царь *TSAR'*
ч	ch as in cheap	CH	читает *chiTAyit*
ш	sh as in show	SH	шапка *SHAPka*
щ	sh as in sheep	SH	щи *SHI*
ъ	hard sign		not pronounced
ь	soft sign		not pronounced

THREE RULES OF PRONUNCIATION

1. Russians pronounce the **o** sound (as in hell**o**) only when it is stressed. When some other vowel is stressed in a word, the letter **o** is pronounced as an **a**. For example, **кот** (*KOT*), but **котá** (*kaTA*). When the letters **е, я,** and sometimes **a** are not stressed they are pronounced **i** as in the English word **it**.

2. Consonants can be hard **ну** (*NU*) or soft **нет** (*NYET*). The soft **n** is like the sound in the word on**i**on. A consonant is hard unless it is followed by a soft vowel letter **я, е, и, ё, ю** or the soft sign **ь**.

3. At the end of a word, or before voiced consonants, **б, в, г, д, ж,** and **з** become their voiceless counterparts, **б → п, в → ф, г → к, д → т, ж → ш, з → с**. Examples: **ход** *KHOT*, **баб** *BAP*, **ног** *NOK*, **автомат** *aftaMAT*, **водка** *VOTka*.

All these changes happen automatically for the native speaker. But if you carefully repeat the examples on the cassette along with the audioscript, you too can sound like a Russian!

TRAVEL TIP

If you have had to change your plans and cannot use your airline ticket, you can apply for a complete refund. Treat your ticket as if it were cash, and return it to your travel agent or to the airline for your money back. Note, however, that some charter tickets are nonrefundable. If you do not use the ticket, you have lost the money, but if you take out special flight insurance, you can collect your refund for that charter ticket from the insuring company.

THE BASICS FOR GETTING BY

MOST FREQUENTLY USED EXPRESSIONS

The expressions in this section are the ones you'll use again and again—fundamental building blocks of conversation, ways to express your wants or needs, and some simple interrogative forms that you can use to construct all sorts of questions. It's a good idea to practice these phrases until you know them by heart.

Hello.	**Здравствуйте.**	*ZDRASTvuytye*
Yes.	**Да.**	*DA*
No.	**Нет.**	*NYET*
Maybe.	**Может быть.**	*MOzhit BYT'*
Please.	**Пожалуйста.**	*paZHAlusta*
Thank you.	**Спасибо.**	*spaSIba*
Thank you very much.	**Большое спасибо.**	*bal'SHOye spaSIba*
Excuse me!	**Извините!**	*izviNItye*
Pardon me!	**Простите!**	*praSTItye*
Make way!	**Дорогу!**	*daROgu*
Watch out! Careful!	**Осторожно!**	*astaROZHna*
Just a minute!	**Минуточку!**	*miNUtachku*
That's all right.	**Хорошо.**	*kharaSHO*
It doesn't matter.	**Ничего.**	*nichiVO*
Good morning.	**Доброе утро.**	*DObraye Utra*
Good afternoon.	**Добрый день.**	*DObry DYEN'*
Good evening.	**Добрый вечер.**	*DObry VYEchir*
Good night.	**Спокойной ночи.**	*spaKOYnay NOchi*

Comrade	**Товарищ** *taVArish*
Mister	**Господин** *gaspaDIN*
Miss, Mrs.	**Госпожа** *gaspaZHA*
Good-bye.	**До свидания.** *da sviDAniya*
Until tomorrow.	**До завтра.** *da ZAFtra*
See you later.	**Пока.** *paKA*
Do you speak English?	**Вы говорите по-английски?** *VY gavaRItye pa-anGLIYski*
I speak a little Russian.	**Я говорю немного по-русски.** *YA gavaRYU niMNOga pa-RUski*
Do you understand?	**Вы понимаете?** *VY paniMAyitye*
I understand.	**Я понимаю.** *YA paniMAyu*
I don't understand.	**Я не понимаю.** *YA NYE paniMAyu*
I'm listening.	**Я слушаю.** *YA SLUshayu*
Speak up!	**Говорите!** *gavaRItye*
What?	**Что?** *SHTO*
What did you say?	**Что вы сказали?** *SHTO VY skaZAli*
How do you say ____	**Как ____** *KAK ____*
■ in Russian?	**по-русски?** *pa-RUski*
What does that mean?	**Что это значит?** *SHTO Eta ZNAchit*
Please repeat.	**Повторите, пожалуйста.** *paftaRItye paZHAlusta*
I'm an American. (*m*)	**Я американец.** *YA amiriKAnits*
I'm an American. (*f*)	**Я американка.** *YA amiriKANka*

Russian often has distinctive forms for men and women. We will use the abbreviation (*m*) to indicate masculine and (*f*) to indicate feminine.

I'm British. (*m*)	**Я англичанин.**	*YA angliCHAnin*
I'm British. (*f*)	**Я англичанка.**	*YA angliCHANka*
I'm Canadian. (*m*)	**Я канадец.**	*YA kaNAdits*
I'm Canadian. (*f*)	**Я канадка.**	*YA kaNATka*
My name is ____ .	**Меня зовут ____ .**	*miNYA zaVUT*
What's your name?	**Как вас зовут?**	*KAK VAS zaVUT*
How are you?	**Как поживаете?**	*KAK pazhiVAyitye*
Fine.	**Хорошо.**	*kharaSHO*
And you?	**А вы?**	*A VY*
Where is ____ ?	**Где ____ ?**	*GDYE*
▪ the bathroom	**туалет**	*tuaLYET*
▪ the entrance	**вход**	*FKHOT*
▪ the exit	**выход**	*VYkhat*
▪ the telephone	**телефон**	*tiliFON*
▪ a taxi	**такси**	*taKSI*
▪ our bus	**наш автобус**	*NASH aFTObus*
Which way did they go?	**Куда они пошли?**	*kuDA aNI paSHLI*
▪ to the right	**направо**	*naPRAva*
▪ to the left	**налево**	*naLYEva*
▪ straight ahead	**прямо**	*PRYAma*
How much does it cost?	**Сколько стоит?**	*SKOL'ka STOit*
I'd like ____ .	**Мне хочется ____ .**	*MNYE KHOchitsa*
Please bring me ____ .	**Принесите мне, пожалуйста ____ .**	*priniSItye MNYE paZHAlusta*
Please show me ____ .	**Покажите мне, пожалуйста ____ .**	*pakaZHYtye MNYE paZHAlusta*
I'm hungry. (*m*)	**Я голоден.**	*YA GOladin*
I'm hungry. (*f*)	**Я голодна.**	*YA galaDNA*
I'm thirsty.	**Мне хочется пить.**	*MNYE KHOchitsa PIT'*

I'm tired. (*m*)	**Я устал.** *YA uSTAL*
I'm tired. (*f*)	**Я устала.** *YA uSTAla*
What's that?	**Что это?** *SHTO Eta*
What's up?	**В чём дело?** *F CHOM DYEla*
What's new?	**Что нового?** *SHTO NOvava*
I (don't) know.	**Я (не) знаю.** *YA (NYE) ZNAyu*

QUESTIONS

Who?	**Кто?** *KTO*
What?	**Что?** *SHTO*
Where?	**Где?** *GDYE*
Where to?	**Куда?** *kuDA*
When?	**Когда?** *kagDA*
Why?	**Почему?** *pachiMU*
How?	**Как?** *KAK*
How much?	**Сколько?** *SKOL'ka*

EXCLAMATIONS

Ouch!	**Ой!** *OY*
That hurts.	**Больно.** *BOL'na*
You're super!	**Молодец!** *malaDYETS*
Darn it!	**Чёрт возьми!** *CHORT vaz'MI*
Well!	**Ну!** *NU*
How beautiful!	**Как красиво!** *KAK kraSIva*
Ugh!	**Фу!** *FU*
That's awful!	**Ужасно!** *uZHASna*
Great! Wonderful!	**Замечательно!** *zamiCHAtil'na*

That's the one!	**Вот это!**	*VOT Eta*
My goodness!	**Боже мой!**	*BOzhe MOY*
Cheers!	**На здоровье!**	*na zdaROvye*
Quiet!	**Тише!**	*TIshe*
Shut up!	**Молчите!**	*malCHItye*
That's enough!	**Хватит!**	*KHVAtit*
Never mind!	**Ничего!**	*nichiVO*
Of course!	**Конечно!**	*kaNYESHna*
With pleasure!	**С удовольствием!**	*s udaVOL'stviyim*
Let's go!	**Пошли!**	*paSHLI*
What a shame!	**Как жаль!**	*KAK ZHAL'*
Nonsense!	**Ерунда!**	*yirunDA*
Are you crazy?	**Вы с ума сошли?**	*VY s uMA saSHLI*
What a fool!	**Какой дурак!**	*kaKOY duRAK*
Good luck!	**Всего хорошего!**	*fsiVO khaROshiva*

PROBLEMS, PROBLEMS, PROBLEMS (EMERGENCIES)

Hurry up!	**Спешите!**	*spiSHYtye*
Look!	**Смотрите!**	*smaTRItye*
Watch out! Be careful!	**Осторожно!**	*astaROZHna*
Listen!	**Слушайте!**	*SLUshaytye*
Wait!	**Подождите!**	*padaZHDItye*
Fire!	**Пожар!**	*paZHAR*
I have lost _____ .(m)	**Я потерял _____ .**	*YA patiRYAL*
I have lost _____ .(f)	**Я потеряла _____ .**	*YA patiRYAla*
■ my suitcase	**мой чемодан**	*MOY chimaDAN*

▓ my pocketbook	**мою сумку** *maYU SUMku*
▓ my briefcase	**мой портфель** *MOY partFYEL'*
I am lost! (*m*)	**Я потерялся!** *YA patiRYALsya*
I am lost! (*f*)	**Я потерялась!** *YA patiRYAlas'*
We're lost.	**Мы потерялись.** *MY patiRYAlis'*
What's the matter with you?	**Что с вами?** *SHTO s VAmi*
What (the devil) do you want?	**Что вам нужно?** *SHTO VAM NUZHna*
Leave me alone!	**Оставьте меня в покое!** *aSTAF'tye miNYA f paKOye*
Go away!	**Пошёл вон!** *paSHOL VON*
Help!	**Помогите!** *pamaGItye*
I'm going to call a cop!	**Я позову милиционера!** *YA pazaVU militsiaNYEra*
Get out!	**Вон!** *VON*
Stop him!	**Задержите его!** *zadirZHYtye yiVO*

He's stolen _____ .	**Он украл.**	*ON uKRAL*
She's stolen _____ .	**Она украла.**	*aNA uKRAla*
 my passport	**мой паспорт**	*MOY PASpart*
my ring	**моё кольцо**	*maYO kal'TSO*
my wallet	**мой бумажник**	*MOY buMAZHnik*
my watch	**мои часы**	*maI chiSY*
Does anyone speak English?	**Кто-нибудь говорит по-английски?**	*KTO-nibut' gavaRIT pa-anGLIYski*
I want to telephone _____ .	**Я хочу позвонить _____ .**	*YA khaCHU pazvaNIT'*
the American Embassy	**в американское посольство.**	*v amiriKANskaye paSOL'stva*
the British Embassy	**в английское посольство**	*v anGLIYskaye paSOL'stva*
the Canadian Embassy	**в канадское посольство**	*v kaNADskaye paSOL'stva*

NUMBERS

If you really want to get around in Russia you will need to know the numbers in Russian. This knowledge is essential for shopping, arranging meetings, ordering tickets, and so on. In a word, knowing the numbers is an essential part of daily communication. The following list contains the cardinal and ordinal numbers along with some other useful quantities.

CARDINAL NUMBERS

0	нуль	NUL'
1	один	aDIN
2	два	DVA
3	три	TRI
4	четыре	chiTYrye
5	пять	PYAT'
6	шесть	SHEST'
7	семь	SYEM'
8	восемь	VOsim'
9	девять	DYEvit'
10	десять	DYEsit'
11	одиннадцать	aDInatsat'
12	двенадцать	dviNAtsat'
13	тринадцать	triNAtsat'
14	четырнадцать	chiTYRnatsat'
15	пятнадцать	pitNAtsat'
16	шестнадцать	shistNAtsat'
17	семнадцать	simNAtsat'
18	восемнадцать	vasimNAtsat'
19	девятнадцать	divitNAtsat'
20	двадцать	DVAtsat'
21	двадцать один	DVAtsat' aDIN
22	двадцать два	DVAtsat' DVA
23	двадцать три	DVAtsat' TRI
24	двадцать четыре	DVAtsat' chiTYrye
25	двадцать пять	DVAtsat' PYAT'
26	двадцать шесть	DVAtsat' SHEST'
27	двадцать семь	DVAtsat' SYEM'

28	двадцать восемь	*DVAtsat' VOsim'*
29	двадцать девять	*DVAtsat' DYEvit'*
30	тридцать	*TRItsat'*
31	тридцать один	*TRItsat' aDIN*
40	сорок	*SOrak*
41	сорок один	*SOrak aDIN*
50	пятьдесят	*pidiSYAT*
60	шестьдесят	*shizdiSYAT*
70	семьдесят	*SYEM'disit*
80	восемьдесят	*VOsim'disit*
90	девяносто	*diviNOSta*
100	сто	*STO*
101	сто один	*STO aDIN*
110	сто десять	*STO DYEsit'*
200	двести	*DVYESti*
300	триста	*TRISta*
400	четыреста	*chiTYrista*
500	пятьсот	*pit'SOT*
600	шестьсот	*shist'SOT*
700	семьсот	*sim'SOT*
800	восемьсот	*vasim'SOT*
900	девятьсот	*divit'SOT*
1000	тысяча	*TYsicha*
2000	две тысячи	*DVYE TYsichi*
5000	пять тысяч	*PYAT' TYsich*
1,000,000	миллион	*miliON*
2,000,000	два миллиона	*DVA miliOna*
5,000,000	пять миллионов	*PYAT' miliOnaf*
1,000,000,000	миллиард	*miliART*

ORDINAL NUMBERS

first	первый	*PYERvy*
second	второй	*ftaROY*
third	третий	*TRYEti*
fourth	четвёртый	*chitVYORty*
fifth	пятый	*PYAty*
sixth	шестой	*shiSTOY*
seventh	седьмой	*sid'MOY*
eighth	восьмой	*vas'MOY*

| ninth | девятый | *diVYAty* |
| tenth | десятый | *diSYAty* |

USEFUL QUANTITIES

a half	половина	*palaVIna*
a quarter	четверть	*CHETvirt'*
ten of a kind	десяток	*diSYAtak*
100 grams	сто грамм	*STO GRAM*
a little bit	немного	*niMNOga*
too little	слишком мало	*SLISHkam MAla*
a little less	поменьше	*paMYEN' she*
a lot	много	*MNOga*
too much	слишком много	*SLISHkam MNOga*
a little more	побольше	*paBOL' she*
a pair	пара	*PAra*
once	один раз	*aDIN RAS*
twice	два раза	*DVA RAza*
many times	много раз	*MNOga RAS*
one more time	ещё раз	*yiSHO RAS*

TRAVEL TIP

You can never really count on Russians having the correct change for the various hard currencies, i.e. dollars, pounds, francs, etc. You should take some cash including small denominations, such as $1- and $5-bills for purchases at hotel bars and for tiny souvenirs. While there is a small commission charge to cash travelers checks, they can be replaced on the spot if lost or stolen. More and more Soviet establishments do accept credit cards. To be absolutely safe bring some combination of cash, travelers checks and a major credit card.

WHEN YOU ARRIVE

PASSPORT CONTROL

When you arrive in Russia you will first proceed to the Passport Control Desk (**Паспортный контроль** *PASpartny kanTROL'*). There your passport and visa will be examined, and after stamping your visa the border guard will return both passport and visa to you. You must then claim your bags on the baggage carousel and pass through customs. There are two lanes. If you having nothing to declare you may proceed through the Green Line (**Зелёный коридор** *ziLYOny kariDOR*). However, since you will probably have some foreign currency, you must pass through the Red Line (**Красный коридор** *KRASny kariDOR*). Here you will hand over your customs declaration form, which contains a list of valuables (jewelry, cameras, etc.) and of currencies and traveler's checks in your possession. **Note that you may not bring Russian rubles into the country.** The customs official may ask to examine your luggage and then will initial and stamp your declaration form and return it to you. Please keep it with you. You will need it to exchange money at authorized bank outlets and you must hand it in upon departure.

Here is my passport.	**Вот мой паспорт.**	*VOT MOY PASpart*
Here is my visa.	**Вот моя виза.**	*VOT maYA VIza*
I'm a tourist.	**Я турист.**	*YA tuRIST*
I'm a businessman.	**Я бизнесмен.**	*YA bisnisMYEN*
I'm on a business trip.	**Я по бизнесу.**	*YA pa BISnisu*
I'll be here for _____ .	**Я здесь буду _____ .**	*YA ZDYES' BUdu*
a few days	**несколько дней**	*NYEskal'ka DNYEY*
a few weeks	**несколько недель**	*NYEskal'ka niDYEL'*
a month	**один месяц**	*aDIN MYEsits*
I'm alone. (*m*)	**Я один.**	*YA aDIN*

T—6
Англ.

Keep for the duration of your stay in the U.S.S.R. or abroad. Not renewable in case of loss.

Persons giving false information in the Customs Declaration, or to Customs officers shall render themselves liable under laws of the U.S.S.R.

CUSTOMS DECLARATION

Full name _____

Citizenship _____

Arriving from _____

Country of 'destination _____

Purpose of visit _____
                  (business, tourism, private, etc.)

My luggage (including hand luggage) submitted for Customs inspection consists of _____ pieces.

With me and in my luggage I have:

  I. Weapons of all descriptions and ammunition _____

  II. Narcotics and appliances for the use thereof _____

  III. Antiques and objects of art (paintings, drawings, icons, sculptures, etc.)_____

IV. U.S.S.R. rubles, U.S.S.R. State Loan bonds, Soviet lottery tickets _____

V. Currency other than U.S.S.R. rubles (bank notes, exchequer bills, coins), payment voucher (cheques, bills, letters of credit, etc.), securities (shares, bonds, etc.) in foreign currencies, precious metals (gold, silver, platinum, metals of platinum group) in any form or condition, crude and processed natural precious stones (diamonds, brilliants, rubies, emeralds, sapphires and pearls), jewelry and other articles made of precious metals and precious stones, and scrap thereof, as well as property papers:

Description	Amount / quantity		For official use
	in figures	in words	
U.S. Dollars			
Pounds Sterling			
French Francs			
Deutschemarks			

VI. U.S.S.R. rubles, other currency, payment vouchers, valuables and any objects belonging to other persons_____

  I am aware that, in addition to the objects listed in the Customs Declaration, I must submit for inspection: printed matter, manuscripts, films, video- and sound recordings, postage stamps, pictorial matter, etc., as well as items not for personal use.

I also declare that my luggage sent separately consists of _____ pieces.

(Date)_____ 198 _____   Owner of luggage _____
                                                                    (signed)

I'm alone. (*f*)	**Я одна.** *YA aDNA*
I'm with my wife.	**Я с женой.** *YA z zhiNOY*
I'm with my husband.	**Я с мужем.** *YA s MUzhim*
I'm with my family.	**Я с семьёй.** *YA s siM'YOY*

CUSTOMS

Here is my declaration.	**Вот моя декларация.** *VOT maYA diklaRAtsiya*
I have nothing to declare.	**Мне нечего декларировать.** *MNYE NYEchiva diklaRIravat'*
These are my suitcases.	**Вот мои чемоданы.** *VOT maI chimaDAny*
These are souvenirs.	**Это сувениры.** *Eta suviNIry*
They are for my personal use.	**Это мои личные вещи.** *Eta maI LICHniye VYEshi*
Do I have to pay duty?	**Мне нужно платить пошлину?** *MNYE NUZHna plaTIT' POSHlinu.*
May I close my bag?	**Можно закрыть чемодан?** *MOZHna zaKRYT' chimaDAN*

BAGGAGE AND PORTERS

When you have cleared customs you will enter the main hall of the airport. If you are with a tourist group or have been invited by a Russian organization, your hosts will probably be waiting for you at the Meeting Point (**Место встречи** *MYESta VSTRYEchi*). If you are traveling alone you should already have a voucher for a hotel room from Intourist. Go directly to the Intourist Desk and ask for help. You might want to take one of the available luggage carts or look for someone to carry your bags.

Where can I find a cart?	**Где можно взять тележку?** *GDYE MOZHna VZYAT' tiLYEZHku*

Porter, please!	**Носильщик, пожалуйста.** *naSIL'shik paZHAlusta*
These are our (my) bags.	**Вот наши (мои) вещи.** *VOT NAshi (maI) VYEshi*
Be careful with this one.	**Осторожно с этим.** *astaROZHna s Etim*

I'll carry this one.	**Этот я сам понесу.** *Etat YA SAM paniSU*
Put them down here.	**Положите их сюда, пожалуйста.** *palaZHYtye IKH syuDA paZHAlusta*
Thank you very much.	**Спасибо большое.** *spaSIba bal'SHOye*
This is for you.	**Вот вам.** *VOT VAM*

AIRPORT TRANSPORTATION

If you are with a group or have been met, transportation to your hotel will be provided. If you are completely on your own, you will probably want to take an official taxi or go with one of the private cars offering livery service. If you do take a private car, make sure you agree on the fare beforehand. The price can vary tremendously. If you already know your way around Moscow there is an inexpensive bus to the River Station (**Речной вокзал** *richNOY vagZAL*) of the Metro. The trip is not that much longer, and the adventure plus your savings make it worthwhile.

Where is our bus?	**Где наш автобус?** *GDYE NASH aFTObus*	
Does this bus go downtown?	**Этот автобус идёт в центр?** *Etat aFTObus iDYOT f TSENTR*	
I want to go to the hotel ____ .	**Я хочу ехать в гостиницу** ____ . *YA khaCHU YEkhat' v gaSTInitsu*	
◼ Cosmos	**Космос** *KOSmas*	
◼ Leningrad	**Ленинград** *lininGRAT*	
◼ Savoy	**Савой** *saVOY*	
How much is the fare?	**Сколько стоит?** *SKOL'ka STOit*	
That's too expensive!	**Это слишком дорого!** *Eta SLISHkam DOraga*	
That's fine. Let's go.	**Хорошо. Поехали.** *kharaSHO paYEkhali*	

TRAVEL TIP

For a special souvenir, you might visit *Mezhnumizmatika*, a joint Russian-West German venture that sells gold and silver coins, commemorative medals, and Soviet gold ingots. The shop located at Pushkinskaya Street 9 in Moscow also has pre-revolutionary banknotes, gold rubles, and proof sets of Soviet and new Russian coins.

BANKING AND MONEY MATTERS

It is illegal to bring Russian currency into the Russian Federation. You must exchange your hard currency or traveler's checks at approved banking facilities. You can do this at your hotel or at the airport. If you need rubles for a taxi or a bus, exchange some funds at the airport. Because you also may not take rubles out of Russia. You must exchange unspent rubles back into a hard currency at the airport prior to departure. In many places goods and services are offered FOR HARD CURRENCY ONLY (**Только на валюту** *TOL'ka na vaLYUtu*). Experienced travelers try not to accumulate rubles toward the end of their stay. The banking facilities are usually open from 9:00 AM to 8:00 PM with a break for lunch.

EXCHANGING CURRENCY

I want to exchange ____ .	**Я хочу обменять** ____ . *YA khaCHU abmiNYAT'*
▪ American dollars	**американские доллары** *amiriKANskiye DOlary*
▪ British pounds	**английские фунты** *anGLIYskiye FUNty*
▪ Canadian dollars	**канадские доллары** *kaNADskiye DOlary*
▪ traveler's checks	**дорожные чеки** *daROZHniye CHEki*
Here is my customs declaration.	**Вот моя декларация.** *VOT maYA diklaRAtsiya*
What is the exchange rate?	**Какой обменный курс?** *kaKOY abMYEny KURS*
Where must I sign?	**Где мне расписаться?** *GDYE MNYE raspiSAtsa*

Large bills if possible.	**Если можно, крупными купюрами.** *YEsli MOZHna KRUPnymi kuPYUrami*
Small bills if possible.	**Если можно, мелькими купюрами.** *YEsli MOZHna MYE|L' kimi kuPYUrami*
Please give me change for this.	**Разменяйте, пожалуйста.** *razmiNYAYtye paZHAlusta*
Give me a receipt please.	**Дайте мне квитанцию, пожалуйста.** *DAYtye MNYE kviTANtsiyu paZHAlusta*

The exchange rate is the same at all official banking points, and exchanging outside of official channels is illegal. The rate fluctuates according to international currency transactions. You must present your passport and your declaration form. To change rubles back into a foreign currency upon departure you will need your original exchange receipt. To keep track of your expenses, you may want to convert the following amounts of rubles to the equivalents in your own currency.

RUSSIAN RUBLES	MY CURRENCY
1	
5	
10	
50	
100	

RUSSIAN MONEY

Russian currency consists of kopecks and rubles. There are one hundred kopecks in a ruble. There are copper-colored coins of 1, 2, 3, and 5 kopecks. Silver-colored coins are available in denominations of 10, 15, 20, and 50 kopecks and one ruble. The size of each coin increases with its value. The bills are color-coded and also increase in size in accordance with value: one ruble—tan; three rubles—green; five rubles—blue; ten rubles—red; twenty-five rubles—violet; fifty rubles—dark green; one hundred rubles—dark brown.

CREDIT CARDS

Most American and European major credit cards are increasingly accepted at hotels and in hotel restaurants, clubs, and bars. You may also use a credit card to pay for purchases at special shops for foreign currency.

Do you accept credit cards?	**Вы принимаете кредитные карточки?** *VY priniMAyitye kriDITniye KARtachki*
I have only this credit card.	**У меня только такая кредитная карточка.** *U miNYA TOL'ka taKAya kriDITnaya KARtachka*
Must I pay in hard currency?	**Надо платить валютой?** *NAda plaTIT' vaLYUtay*
May I pay cash?	**Можно платить наличными?** *MOZHna plaTIT' naLICHnymi*

BANKING

Currently, foreign organizations and individuals may have an account with an ever increasing number of banks.

I would like to open an account.	**Я хочу открыть счёт.**	*YA khaCHU atKRYT' SHOT*
I want to make a deposit.	**Я хочу выдать вклад.**	*YA khaCHU VYdat' FKLAT*
I want to make a withdrawal.	**Я хочу принять вклад.**	*YA khaCHU priNYAT' FKLAT*
I need a deposit slip.	**Мне нужен приходный ордер.** *MNYE NUzhin priKHODny ORdir*	
I need a withdrawal slip.	**Мне нужен расходный ордер.** *MNYE NUzhin rasKHODny ORdir*	

TIPPING

If a service charge is already included in your restaurant check, you might leave the small change that is returned to you. For small courtesies you can leave a 100 ruble note with the coatroom or restroom attendant. Tip porters a dollar for one or two large suitcases. Other people who perform personal services will welcome a sign of your appreciation. A pack of foreign cigarettes often can be substituted for a cash tip.

AT THE HOTEL

If you are traveling with a group, your hotel arrangements will have already been made through one of the many travel organizations. Individuals who have confirmed hotel reservations will have a prepaid voucher from their travel agent. If you are being met by an official organization, it will have arranged accommodations. When you arrive at the airport, go directly to the Intourist Desk or meet your hosts.

GETTING TO YOUR HOTEL

Here is my voucher.	**Вот мой ваучер.**	*VOT MOY VAUchir*
At which hotel will I be staying?	**В какой гостинице я буду?**	*F kaKOY gaSTInitse YA BUdu*
I want to go to the hotel ____ .	**Я хочу поехать в гостиницу ____ .**	*YA khaCHU paYEkhat' v gaSTInitsu*
▪ Cosmos	**Космос**	*KOSmas*
▪ International	**Международная**	*mizhdunaRODnaya*
▪ Intourist	**Интурист**	*intuRIST*
▪ Leningrad	**Ленинград**	*lininGRAT*
▪ Metropole	**Метрополь**	*mitraPOL'*
▪ National	**Националь**	*natsiaNAL'*
▪ Baltic	**Прибалтийская**	*pribalTIYskaya*
▪ Russia	**Россия**	*raSIya*
Is it far?	**Она далеко?**	*aNA daliKO*
Is it near?	**Она близко?**	*aNA BLISka*
What's the number of my bus?	**Какой номер моего автобуса?**	*kaKOY NOmir mayiVO aFTObusa*
What's the number of my car?	**Какой номер моей машины?**	*kaKOY NOmir maYEY maSHYny*

CHECKING IN

When you arrive at the hotel you must present your passport with visa, which will be retained for a day or two for official registration. You will receive a key card (**пропуск** *PROpusk*) to present at the front door and either at the desk in the main lobby or on your floor to obtain your room key. Please leave your key at either desk when you go out for the day or evening.

I reserved a single room.	**Я забронировал номер на одного.** *YA zabraNIraval NOmir na adnaVO*
We need a double room.	**Нам нужен номер на двоих.** *NAM NUzhin NOmir na dvaIKH*
I reserved a deluxe room.	**Я забронировал номер люкс.** *YA zabraNIraval NOmir LYUKS*
Where can I get the key?	**Где мне взять ключ?** *GDYE MNYE VZYAT' KLYUCH*

When can I pick up my passport?	**Когда можно получить паспорт?** *kagDA MOZHna paluCHIT' PASpart*
On what floor is my room?	**На каком этаже мой номер?** *na kaKOM etaZHE MOY NOmir*
Where is the elevator?	**Где лифт?** *GDYE LIFT*
Where is the service bureau?	**Где Бюро обслуживания?** *GDYE byuRO apSLUzhivaniya*
When is the restaurant open?	**Когда ресторан открыт?** *kagDA ristaRAN atKRYT*
Is there a snack bar on the floor?	**Есть буфет на этаже?** *YEST' buFYET na etaZHE*
Do I need a ticket for breakfast?	**Мне нужен талон на завтрак?** *MNYE NUzhin taLON na ZAFtrak*

ON YOUR FLOOR

You may have a "key lady" (**дежурная** *diZHURnaya*) who sits at a desk on your floor and can provide you with a key. She will also bring you tea, wake you up, arrange for minor repairs, and provide extra soap, towels, and the like. In brief, she can do many things to make your life easier.

Hello! My name is ___	**Здравствуйте! Меня зовут ___ .** *ZDRASTvuytye miNYA zaVUT*
My key, please.	**Мой ключ, пожалуйста.** *MOY KLYUCH paZHAlusta*
Room No. 5.	**Номер пять.** *NOmir PYAT'*
Room No. 16.	**Номер шестнадцать.** *NOmir shistNAtsat'*

You need not say the entire number for your room, such as 1420, 719, 633. Instead you can use the last two digits of the room number on that floor.

Please bring me ____ .	**Принесите мне, пожалуйста ____ .** *priniSItye MNYE paZHAlusta*
an ashtray	**пепельницу** *PYEpil' nitsu*
a bar of soap	**кусок мыла** *kuSOK MYla*
a blanket	**одеяло** *adiYAla*
some boiling water	**кипяток** *kipiTOK*
a bottle of mineral water	**бутылку минеральной воды** *buTYLku miniRAL'nay vaDY*
a cot	**раскладушку** *rasklaDUSHku*
some envelopes	**конверты** *kanVYERty*
a glass of tea	**стакан чая** *staKAN CHAya*
another pillow	**ещё подушку** *yiSHO paDUSHku*
some postcards	**открытки** *atKRYTki*
another towel	**ещё полотенце** *yiSHO palaTYENtse*
more hangers	**ещё вешалки** *yiSHO VYEshalki*
some toilet paper	**туалетную бумажку** *tuaLYETnuyu buMAZHku*
writing paper	**бумагу для писем** *buMAgu dlya PIsim*
Just a minute!	**Минуточку!** *miNUtachku*
Come in!	**Входите!** *fkhaDItye*
Please place it there.	**Положите, пожалуйста, туда.** *palaZHYtye paZHAlusta tuDA*
Please wake me at ____ .	**Разбудите меня ____ .** *razbuDItye miNYA*
6:00 AM	**в шесть часов** *f SHEST' chiSOF*
6:30 AM	**в половине седьмого** *f palaVInye sid'MOva*
7:00 AM	**в семь часов** *f SYEM' chiSOF*
7:30 AM	**в половине восьмого** *f palaVInye vas'MOva*
Where can I press ____ ?	**Где можно гладить ____ ?** *GDYE MOZHna GLAdit'*

Can you repair ___ ?	**Вы можете чинить ___ ?** *VY MOzhitye chiNIT'*
Can you wash ___ ?	**Вы можете стирать ___ ?** *VY MOzhitye stiRAT'*
▦ my dress	**моё платье** *maYO PLAt' ye*
▦ my jacket	**мой пиджак** *MOY pidZHAK*
▦ my shirts	**мои рубашки** *maI ruBASHki*
▦ my slacks	**мои штаны** *maI shtaNY*
▦ my socks	**мои носки** *maI naSKI*
▦ my suit	**мой костюм** *MOY kaSTYUM*

COMPLAINTS

There is no ___ .	**Нет ___ .** *NYET*
▦ cold water	**холодной воды** *khaLODnay vaDY*
▦ hot water	**горячей воды** *gaRYAchey vaDY*
___ doesn't work.	**___ не работает.** *NYE raBOtayit*
▦ The faucet	**Смеситель** *smiSItil'*
▦ The lamp	**Лампа** *LAMpa*
▦ The plug	**Розетка** *raZYETka*
▦ The radio	**Радио** *RAdio*
▦ The refrigerator	**Холодильник** *khalaDIL'nik*
▦ The sink	**Умывальник** *umyVAL'nik*
▦ The shower	**Душ** *DUSH*
▦ The switch	**Выключатель** *vyklyuCHAtil'*
▦ The telephone	**Телефон** *tiliFON*
▦ The television	**Телевизор** *tiliVIzar*
▦ The toilet	**Унитаз** *uniTAS*
It's too cold in my room.	**В номере слишком холодно.** *v NOmirye SLISHkam KHOladna*

It's too hot in my room.	**В номере слишком жарко.** *v NOmirye SLISHkam ZHARka*
The window doesn't open.	**Окно не открывается.** *akNO NYE atkryVAyitsa*
The window doesn't close.	**Окно не закрывается.** *akNO NYE zakryVAyitsa*
The room hasn't been cleaned.	**Номер не убран.** *NOmir NYE Ubran*

HOTEL SERVICES AND SIGNS

You will probably see some of the following signs in your hotel

Administrator	**АДМИНИСТРАТОР** *adminiSTRAtar*
Bank	**БАНК** *BANK*
Bar	**БАР** *BAR*
Barber Shop/Beauty Salon	**ПАРИКМАХЕРСКАЯ** *parikMAkhirskaya*
Beriozka Store	**БЕРЁЗКА** *biRYOSka*
Cafe	**КАФЕ** *kaFYEY*
Cashier	**КАССА** *KAsa*
Checkroom	**КАМЕРА ХРАНЕНИЯ** *KAmira khraNYEniya*
Coatroom	**ГАРДЕРОБ** *gardiROP*
Currency Exchange	**ОБМЕННЫЙ ПУНКТ** *abMYEny PUNKT*
Emergency Exit	**ЗАПАСНЫЙ ВЫХОД** *zaPASny VYkhat*
Information	**ИНФОРМАЦИЯ** *infarMAtsiya*
Lunch Break	**ПЕРЕРЫВ** *piriRYF*
Newspaper Stand	**ГАЗЕТНЫЙ КИОСК** *gaZYETny kiOSK*

Nightclub	**НОЧНОЙ БАР** *nachNOY BAR*
No Vacancy	**МЕСТ НЕТ** *MYEST NYET*
Passport Desk	**ПАСПОРТНЫЙ СТОЛ** *PASpartny STOL*
Post office	**ПОЧТА** *POCHta*
Reception Room	**ПРИЁМНАЯ** *priYOMnaya*
Restaurant	**РЕСТОРАН** *ristaRAN*
Restroom (men's)	**МУЖСКОЙ ТУАЛЕТ** *mushSKOY tuaLYET*
(ladies')	**ЖЕНСКИЙ ТУАЛЕТ** *ZHENsky tuaLYET*
Sauna	**САУНА** *SAUna*
Service Bureau	**БЮРО ОБСЛУЖИВАНИЯ** *byuRO apSLUzhivaniya*
Snack Bar	**БУФЕТ** *buFYET*
Souvenirs	**СУВЕНИРЫ** *suviNIry*
Swimming Pool	**БАССЕЙН** *baSYEYN*
Theater Desk	**ТЕАТРАЛЬНЫЙ СТОЛ** *tiaTRAL'ny STOL*

CHECKING OUT

I'm departing today.	**Я сегодня уезжаю.** *YA siVODnya uyiZHAyu*
When is check-out time?	**Когда расчётный час?** *kagDA rasSHOTny CHAS*
Please order a taxi for me.	**Закажите мне такси, пожалуйста.** *zakaZHYtye MNYE taKSI paZHAlusta*
How will you be paying?	**Как вы будете платить?** *KAK VY BUditye plaTIT'*

Do you accept rubles?	**Вы работаете на рубли?** *VY raBOtayitye na ruBLI*
No, only foreign currency.	**Нет, только на валюту.** *NYET TOL'ka na vaLYUtu*
I'll pay with a credit card.	**Я плачу кредитной карточкой.** *YA plaCHU kriDITnay KARtachkay*
I left my suitcase in the room.	**Я оставил чемодан в номере.** *YA aSTAvil chimaDAN v NOmirye*
Let the bellboy bring it down.	**Пусть швейцар принесёт.** *PUST' shviyTSAR priniSYOT*

TRAVEL TIP

Touring on the cheap? You can save on many daily expenses by avoiding the convenient tourist outlets where hard currency is often required. If you use rubles to buy your theater tickets at a kiosk and your meals at a Russian snack bar or restaurant outside of your hotel, you will spend only a fraction of the cost in dollars or pounds. Use your rubles for books and records at local Russian stores. A final tip to save money: use the Metro for transportation around the city. You avoid the traffic, save money, and treat yourself to an excursion through the magnificent underground architecture of many Metro stations.

GETTING AROUND TOWN

If you really want to explore the country, get out and about on your own. You'll certainly want to walk along some of the busier streets, and you should also be familiar with the excellent systems of public transportation in most major cities.

THE METRO

In Moscow, St. Petersburg, and other large cities you absolutely must try out the subway (**Метро**   *miTRO*). The system is clean and very inexpensive, and many of the stations themselves are architectural masterpieces. You can find the Metro by the big red capital **M**. The trains run from 6:00 AM until approximately 1:00 AM, but you will want to get on your last train around midnight. The trains run with very short intervals, sometimes as little as thirty seconds during rush hour. Moscow has the most extensive system, based on a circular main line (**Кольцевая линия** *kal'tsiVAya LIniya*). Several lines intersect the circle and meet at various places near the middle of the city. Each station has a large map, and you can find a map inside each subway car. On the wall you will see a complete listing of the stations on your particular line. To enter the subway you must deposit a token in the automatic gates. You can purchase a token (**жетон**) at the cashier's booth (**Касса**   *KAsa*), or your might purchase a monthly pass (**единый билет**   *yiDIny biLYET*), which permits you to use any public transportation. If you have such a card you should show it to an attendant standing near an open gate.

Where is the nearest ___ ?	**Где ближайшая ___ ?** *GDYE bliZHAYshaya*
◼ subway station	**станция метро** *STANtsiya miTRO*
How can I get to ___ ?	**Как проехать ___ ?** *KAK praYEkhat'*
◼ downtown	**в центр** *f TSENTR*

■ Red Square	**на Красную площадь**	*na KRASnuyu PLOshat'*
■ Moscow University	**в МГУ**	*v EM GA U*
■ the Hotel Rossiya	**в гостиницу Россия**	*v gaSTInitsu raSIya*
How many more stops?	**Сколько ещё остановок?**	*SKOL'ka yiSHO astaNOvak*
Where should I get off?	**Где мне выйти?**	*GDYE MNYE VYti*
Do I have to transfer?	**Мне надо пересесть?**	*MNYE NAda piriSYEST'*
Please tell me when to get off.	**Скажите, пожалуйста, когда мне выйти.**	*skaZHYtye paZHAlusta kagDA MNYE VYti*
Careful, the doors are closing.	**Осторожно, двери закрываются.**	*astaROZHna DVYEri zakryVAyutsa*

You will see several signs inside the Metro. You should know what they mean.

Don't lean against the doors	**Не прислоняться**	*NYE prislaNYAtsa*
Entrance	**Вход**	*FKHOT*
Exit to the city	**Выход в город**	*VYkhat v GOrat*
No entrance	**Нет входа**	*NYET FKHOda*
Reserved for	**Место для**	*MYEsta dlya*
■ the handicapped	**инвалидов**	*invaLIdaf*
■ the elderly	**лиц пожилого возраста**	*LITS pazhyLOva VOZrasta*
■ and passengers with children	**и пассажиров с детьми**	*I pasaZHYraf z dit'MI*
Transfer	**Переход**	*piriKHOT*

TRAMS, TROLLEYBUSES, BUSES

You are likely to encounter trams or trolley cars that run on tracks (**трамвай** *tramVAY*), trolleybuses that have tires but are connected overhead to electric cables (**троллейбус** *traLYEYbus*), and regular buses (**автобус** *aFTObus*). You can use a monthly pass or purchase a book of tickets (**проездные билеты** *prayizNYye biLYEty*) at most streetcorner kiosks. In many cities the honor system is in effect, and you must stamp your ticket in a ticket punch (**компостер** *kamPOStir*) or put your coins in the cash box and tear off a ticket. Spot checks are made, and if you do not have a valid ticket you will be subject to a fine and a brief lecture on social responsibility. If you lack the correct change you might ask your fellow passengers to help. All trams, trolleybuses, and buses are identified by a number.

Where is the nearest ____ stop?	**Где ближайшая остановка ____ ?** *GDYE bliZHAYshaya astaNOFka*
▮ tram	**трамвая** *tramVAya*
▮ trolleybus	**троллейбуса** *traLYEYbusa*
▮ bus	**автобуса** *aFTObusa*
How much is the fare?	**Сколько стоит проезд?** *SKOL'ka STOit praYEST*
What is the next stop?	**Какая следующая остановка?** *kaKAya SLYEduyushaya astaNOFka*
Does this bus go to ____ ?	**Этот автобус идёт до ____ ?** *Etat aFTObus iDYOT da*
▮ the Bolshoi Theater	**Большого театра** *bal'SHOva tiAtra*
▮ the Hermitage	**Эрмитажа** *ermiTAzha*
How many more stops?	**Сколько ещё остановок?** *SKOL'ka yiSHO astaNOvak*
Are you getting off?	**Вы выходите?** *VY vyKHOditye*
A book of tickets, please.	**Абонементную книжку, пожалуйста.** *abaniMYENTnuyu KNISHku paZHAlusta*

Punch my ticket, please.	**Пробейте, пожалуйста.** *praBYEYtye paZHAlusta*
Can you give me change?	**Не разменяйте?** *NYE razmiNYAYtye*

TAXIS

Metered taxis can also transport you at very reasonable prices, but it is not always easy to find a free one. A little green lamp in the windshield indicates that the taxi is free. You may hail a taxi on the street or seek out the nearest cab stand, marked by a capital T on a checkered background. In addition to metered taxis, many private car operators (**частники** *CHASniki*) are willing to take you to your destination for a few rubles. Be sure to agree on the fare ahead of time.

Is there a taxi stand near by?	**Есть поблизости стоянка такси?** *YEST' paBLIzasti staYANka taKSI*
Are you free?	**Вы свободны?** *VY svaBODny*
I want to go _____ .	**Я хочу поехать _____ .** *YA khaCHU paYEkhat'*
▪ to the airport	**в аэропорт** *v aeraPORT*
▪ to this address	**в этот адрес** *v Etat Adris*
▪ to the hotel	**в гостиницу** *v gaSTInitsu*
▪ to Kiev Station	**на Киевский вокзал** *NA KIyivski vagZAL*
▪ to the Kremlin	**в Кремль** *F KRYEML'*
How much does it cost?	**Сколько стоит?** *SKOL'ka STOit*
Faster. I'm late.	**Быстрее. Я опаздываю.** *bySTRYEye YA aPAZdyvayu*
A little slower, please.	**Помедленее, пожалуйста.** *paMYEdliniye paZHAlusta*
Stop here.	**Остановитесь здесь.** *astanaVItyes' ZDYES'*

Go straight.	**Прямо.** *PRYAma*
To the right.	**Направо.** *naPRAva*
To the left.	**Налево.** *naLYEva*
Is it still far?	**Ещё далеко?** *yiSHO daliKO*
Please wait for me.	**Подождите меня, пожалуйста.** *padaZHDItye miNYA paZHAlusta*
How much do I owe?	**Сколько с меня?** *SKOL'ka s miNYA*
This is for you.	**Это для вас.** *Eta dlya VAS*

SIGHTSEEING

Where is the service bureau?	**Где Бюро обслуживания?** *GDYE byuRO apSLUzhivaniya*
Where is the excursion office?	**Где Экскурсионное бюро?** *GDYE ekskursiOnaye byuRO*
I need an interpreter.	**Мне нужен переводчик.** *MNYE NUzhin piriVOTchik*

How much does it cost _____ ?	**Сколько стоит _____ ?** *SKOL'ka STOit*
▦ for an hour	**за час** *za CHAS*
▦ for a day	**за день** *za DYEN'*
There are two (three, four) of us.	**Нас двое (трое, четверо).** *NAS DVOye (TROye, CHETvira)*
Where can I buy _____ ?	**Где мне купить _____ ?** *GDYE MNYE kuPIT'*
▦ a guide book	**путеводитель** *putivaDItil'*
▦ a map of the city	**план города** *PLAN GOrada*
▦ a phrase book	**разговорник** *razgaVORnik*
Is there a city tour?	**Есть экскурсия по городу?** *YEST' ekSKURsiya pa GOradu*
What are the main attractions?	**Какие главные достопримечательности?** *kaKIye GLAVniye dastaprimiCHAtil'nasti*
Where does it leave from?	**Откуда отправляется?** *atKUda atpravLYAyitsa*
We would like to see _____ .	**Мы бы хотели смотреть _____ .** *MY BY khaTYEli smaTRYET'*
▦ the Bolshoi Theater	**Большой театр** *bal'SHOY tiATR*
▦ Red Square	**Красную площадь** *KRASnuyu PLOshat'*
▦ the Kremlin	**Кремль** *KRYEML'*
▦ Moscow University	**МГУ** *EM GA U*
▦ GUM (the department store)	**ГУМ** *GUM*
▦ Children's World	**Детский Мир** *DYETski MIR*
▦ the Aurora	**Аврору** *avROru*
▦ the Winter Palace	**Зимний дворец** *ZIMni dvaRYETS*
▦ the Armory	**Оружейную палату** *aruZHEYnuyu paLAtu*
▦ a market	**рынок** *RYnak*

▦ the cathedral	**собор**	*saBOR*
▦ the cemetery	**кладбище**	*KLADbishe*
▦ the city hall	**городской совет**	*garatSKOY saVYET*
▦ a church	**церковь**	*TSERkaf'*
▦ the concert hall	**концертный зал**	*kanTSERTny ZAL*
▦ the gardens	**сады**	*saDY*
▦ the institute	**институт**	*instiTUT*
▦ the library	**библиотеку**	*bibliaTYEku*
▦ the monastery	**монастырь**	*manaSTYR'*
▦ the monument	**памятник**	*PAmitnik*
▦ the museum	**музей**	*muZYEY*
▦ the river	**реку**	*RYEku*
▦ the stadium	**стадион**	*stadiON*
▦ the tower	**башню**	*BASHnyu*
▦ the zoo	**зоопарк**	*zaaPARK*

Is it open?	**Открыто?**	*atKRYta*
Is it closed?	**Закрыто?**	*zaKRYta*
What is the admission price?	**Сколько стоит билет?**	*SKOL'ka STOit biLYET*
May I take photos?	**Можно фотографировать?**	*MOZHna fatagraFIravat'*

A SIGHTSEEING ITINERARY

Russia has a rich history and culture. In addition to the major cities of Russia, Moscow and St. Petersburg, there are dozens of other cities and villages with a splendid architectural tradition. You also should not miss the opportunity to sample the great variety of cultures and cuisines of the individual republics, each of which has its own distinctive character. What follows is merely a sketch—a broad overview of some places in Moscow and

St. Petersburg that you might want to see if they are not included in your tour, or if you are traveling on your own and designing your own sightseeing schedule.

MOSCOW

Begin your visit to Moscow with an excursion around the city (**экскурсия по городу** *ekSKURsiya pa GOradu*), now the capital of the Union of Soviet Socialist Republics. Here the old mixes with the new, and nowhere is the combination more apparent than on Red Square (**Красная площадь** *KRASnaya PLOshat'*) and in the Kremlin (**Кремль** *KRYEML'*). Once the stronghold of the Russian tsars and highlighted by magnificent cathedrals, including the landmark St. Basil's, the square was the center of world attention for the parades on May Day (May 1) and the Anniversary of the Revolution (November 7). Here is the famous Lenin Mausoleum (**Мавзолей Ленина** *mavzaLYEY LYEnina*). Inside the Kremlin walls is the seat of the Russian government, along with the famous Palace of Congresses (**Дворец съездов** *dvaRYETS SYEZdaf*), often open to the public for ballet and opera performances. Here too is the famous Armory (**Оружейная палата** *aruZHEYnaya paLAta*), now a museum celebrating Russia's regal past. There is also an opportunity to see the diamond collection, the Russian Crown Jewels (**Алмазный Фонд** *alMAZny FONT*). Turning to modern Moscow, you might want to see the Exhibition of National Economic Achievements—VDNKh for short (**ВДНХ**). Among the most famous museums here are the Tretyakov Gallery (**Третьяковская галерея** *trit'yaKOFskaya galiRYEya*) and the Pushkin Museum, with excellent collections of Western art. You can visit the Television Tower at Ostankino for an unparalleled view of the city. Another favorite spot for photos is near Moscow University, overlooking the Moscow River. Often you will see newlyweds who come here for a picture-taking session.

Should you wish to get out into the countryside, a day trip can bring you to the estate of Leo Tolstoy at Yasnaya Polyana. Another worthwhile destination is the town of Sergiev Posad, where the Russian Orthodox Church keeps alive century-old traditions. Here you'll find an Orthodox seminary and working cathedrals, along with the final resting place of Boris Godunov. For a change of pace you might want to visit the home of the Soviet cosmonauts (**космонавты** *kasmaNAFty*) at Star City (**Звёздны** *ZVYOZny*).

ST. PETERSBURG

Created as a "window to Europe" by Peter the Great in the first part of the eighteenth century, St. Petersburg — then Leningrad as it was named — quickly became capital and architectural showplace of the Russian empire. No expense was spared on the palaces, ministries, and churches that adorn the center of the city. Crisscrossed by numerous canals, it is a true "Venice of the North." The city has a wealth of attractions: the Palace Square, site of the storming of the Winter Palace (**Зимний дворец** *ZIMni dvaRYETS*), the Peter and Paul Fortress (**Петропавловская крепость** *pitraPAVlafskaya KRYEpast'*), the Russian Mint, and the Peter and Paul Cathedral, which became the resting place of the Romanov emperors. The dark side of Russian history can be seen in the fortress cells where Dostoevsky and other leading intellectuals were once imprisoned. Here at the Smolny Institute, the first school for women in Russia, Lenin planned the revolution that changed the face of the Russian Empire in the twentieth century. Do not miss the Hermitage (**Эрмитаж** *ermiTASH*), second only to the Louvre in Paris for its collection of art. You might also visit some of the other residences of the tsarist family, Peter the Great's country palace with its magnificent fountains (**Петродворец** *pitradvaRYETS*) or the stately homes at Pushkino (**Пушкино**) and Pavlovsk (**Павловск**).

To see Old Russia, you might plan a trip to Suzdal (**Суздаль**), a city preserved as a museum of Russian architecture. Here you will be treated to Russian meals baked and served in clay pots, along with a taste of Russian mead (**медовуха** *midaVUkha*).

RELIGIOUS SERVICES

Many of the hundreds of Russian Orthodox churches built prior to the revolution of 1917 are again open. If you want to attend an Orthodox service you must find an active church (**действующая церковь** *DYEYSTvuyushaya TSERkaf'*). Ask at the service bureau in your hotel or contact your embassy for times and places of religious services.

Is there ___ nearby?	**Есть поблизости ___ ?** *YEST' paBLIzasti*
▦ a Catholic church	**католический костёл** *kataLIchiski kaSTYOL*
▦ a Protestant church	**протестантская церковь** *pratiSTANTskaya TSERkaf'*
▦ an Orthodox church	**православная церковь** *pravaSLAVnaya TSERkaf'*
▦ a mosque	**мечеть** *miCHET'*
▦ synagogue	**синагога** *sinaGOga*
At what time is the service?	**Когда служба?** *kagDA SLUZHba*
I would like to speak with ___ .	**Я хотел бы поговорить ___ .** *YA khaTYEL BY pagavaRIT'*
▦ a priest	**со священником** *sa sviSHEnikam*
▦ a minister	**с пастором** *s PAStaram*
▦ a rabbi	**с раввином** *s raVInam*

TRAVEL TIP

Russians almost always carry a net bag (**сеточка** *SYEtachka*) or a plastic bag when they go out for the day: they call it an **авоська** *aVOS'ka*, meaning "just in case." Most items are not packaged, and you will not receive free bags in most stores.

PLANNING A TRIP

During your stay you may want to plan a trip to additional places of interest. You can travel throughout Russia by plane, train, ship, bus, or car.

AIR TRAVEL

Where is the check-in counter?	**Где регистрация?** *GDYE rigiSTRAtsiya*
When is there a flight to _____ ?	**Когда полёт в _____ ?** *kagDA paLYOT v*
St. Petersburg	**Санкт-Петербург** *SANKT pitirBURK*
Riga	**Ригу** *RIgu*
Toshkent	**Ташкент** *tashKYENT*
Tbilisi	**Тбилиси** *tbiLIsi*
A one way ticket to _____ .	**Один билет до _____ .** *aDIN biLYET da*
Irkutsk	**Иркутска** *irKUTska*
Kiev	**Киева** *KIyiva*
A round trip ticket.	**Туда и обратно.** *tuDA I aBRATna*
A seat _____ .	**Место _____ .** *MYESta*
next to the window	**у окна** *u akNA*
on the aisle	**у прохода** *u praKHOda*
in the smoking section	**в салоне для курящих** *f saLOnye dlya kuRYAshikh*
in the non-smoking section	**в салоне для некурящих** *f saLOnye dlya nikuRYAshikh*
in first class	**в первом классе** *f PYERvam KLAsye*
in business class	**в бизнес классе** *v BIZnis KLAsye*
in economy (tourist) class	**в туристическом классе** *f turiSTIchiskam KLAsye*

What does the ticket cost?	**Сколько стоит билет?** *SKOL'ka STOit biLYET*
Will a meal be served?	**Кормить будут?** *karMIT' BUdut*
When does the aircraft depart?	**Когда вылетает самолёт?** *kagDA VYlitayit samaLYOT*
When does it arrive?	**Когда прибывает?** *kagDA pribyVAyit*
How long is the flight?	**Сколько времени длится полёт?** *SKOL'ka VRYEmini DLItsa paLYOT*
I'll check this suitcase.	**Этот чемодан я сдаю в багаж.** *Etat chimaDAN YA ZDAyu v baGASH*
What is our flight number?	**Какой номер нашего рейса?** *kaKOY NOmir NAshiva RYEYsa*
This is your boarding pass.	**Вот посадочный талон.** *VOT paSAdachny taLON*
This your baggage claim check.	**Вот багажная бирка.** *VOT baGAZHnaya BIRka*
Please confirm my reservation.	**Потвердите моё бронирование.** *patvirDItye maYO braNIravaniya*
We are now boarding.	**Объявляется посадка.** *abyavLYAyitsa paSATka*
Please check these ____ .	**Проверьте, пожалуйста, эти ____ .** *praVYER'tye paZHAlusta Eti*
films	**плёнки** *PLYONki*
computer disks	**компьютерные диски** *kamPYUtirniye DISki*
Please do not X-ray them.	**Не просветьте, пожалуйста.** *NYE praSVYET'tye paZHAlusta*

Note: Airport security X-ray machines have become increasingly sensitive, and most will not damage your film. To be on the safe side, you might have computer disks and valuable photographic memories checked by hand. You can always ask politely. If the attendant refuses, bow to his wishes.

SHIPBOARD TRAVEL

Where is the dock?	**Где пристань?** *GDYE PRIstan'*
When does the next boat leave for ____ ?	**Когда следующий теплоход до ____ ?** *kagDA SLYEduyushi tiplaKHOT da*
How long does the trip take?	**Сколько времени в пути?** *SKOL'ka VRYEmini f puTI*
When do we land?	**Когда мы приплываем?** *kagDA MY priplyVAyim*
When do we sail?	**Когда мы отплываем?** *kagDA MY atplyVAyim*
A first class ticket.	**Билет первого класса.** *biLYET PYERvava KLAsa*
A tourist class ticket.	**Билет туристического класса.** *biLYET turiSTIchiskava KLAsa*
I would like a cabin.	**Я хотел бы каюту.** *YA khaTYEL BY kaYUtu*
I don't feel well.	**Мне плохо.** *MNYE PLOkha*

| Do you have anything for sea sickness? | **Есть у вас что-нибудь от морской болезни?** *YEST' u VAS SHTO-nibut' at marSKOY baLYEZni* |

TRAIN SERVICE

Traveling by train can be a pleasant way to go between cities. The overnight trains between Moscow and St. Petersburg or other cities offer an opportunity to make acquaintances, avoid weather delays at airports, and get a good night's sleep. Moscow has several train stations, which serve different destinations. Be sure to ask from which station your train departs.

| I want to get to ____ . | **Мне на ____ .** *MNYE na* |

■ Kazan Station	**Казанский вокзал** *kaZANski vagZAL*
■ Kiev Station	**Киевский вокзал** *KIyifski vagZAL*
■ Leningrad Station	**Ленинградский вокзал** *lininGRATski vagZAL*
■ Riga Station	**Рижский вокзал** *RISHki vagZAL*
■ Yaroslav Station	**Ярославский вокзал** *yaraSLAFski vagZAL*

A first class ticket.	**Билет в мягком вагоне.** *biLYET v MYAkam vaGOnye*
A second class ticket.	**Билет в купейном вагоне.** *biLYET v kuPYEYnam vaGOnye*
A round trip ticket please.	**Обратный билет, пожалуйста.** *aBRATny biLYET paZHAlusta*
A non-smoking compartment.	**Купе для некурящих.** *kuPE dlya nikuRYAshikh*
When does the train leave?	**Когда отправляется поезд?** *kagDA atpravLYAyitsa POyist*
From what platform?	**С какой платформы?** *s kaKOY platFORmy*
Where is Car # ____ ?	**Где вагон номер ____ ?** *GDYE vaGON NOmir*

Where is my seat/berth?	**Где моё место?**	*GDYE maYO MYESta*
Is there a dining car?	**Есть вагон-ресторан?**	*YEST' vaGON ristaRAN*
Bring us some tea, please.	**Принесите нам чаю, пожалуйста.** *priniSItye NAM CHAyu paZHAlusta*	
Where are we now?	**Где мы сейчас?**	*GDYE MY siCHAS*
Will we arrive on schedule?	**Мы прибываем по расписанию?** *MY pribyVAyim pa raspiSAniyu*	
Are we late?	**Мы опаздываем?**	*MY aPAZdyvayim*

TRAVEL TIP

If you are traveling on your own, finding a restaurant and ordering a meal can be time consuming. You can probably get a cup of coffee, juice, and rolls or pastries for breakfast at your hotel buffet. For a delicious lunch without a wait, try the smorgasbord (**Шведский стол** *SHVETski STOL*) available for a few dollars at one of the hotels for foreigners. In the evening you might do as Russians do and eat at the theater buffet. You should go early (at least forty-five minutes before the performance) to avoid the rush and the lines. It might result in a new acquaintance and a conversation.

ENTERTAINMENT AND DIVERSIONS

BALLET, CONCERTS, MOVIES, OPERA

No trip to Russia is complete without a visit to the theater. If you are with a group, a theater visit is probably included in your schedule. If you are on your own, you can order tickets through the theater desk in your hotel. You may also find a ticket at one of the many theater ticket kiosks throughout the city. If you suddenly find that your evening is free you might try to purchase a cancellation ticket by going to the theater about an hour before the performance. The most famous of Moscow's theaters is, of course, the Bolshoi (**Большой театр** *bal'SHOY tiATR*) —home to an opera and a ballet company. The Bolshoi Ballet often performs in the Palace of Congresses (**Дворец съездов**) *dvaRYETS SYEZdaf*) in the Kremlin. You can also see opera and ballet in Moscow at the Stanislavsky Musical Theater (**Музыкальный театр имени Станиславского** *muzyKAL'ny tiATR Imini staniSLAFskava*). An opportunity overlooked by some tourists is the Operetta Theater (**Театр оперетты** *tiATR apiRYEty*), which performs Russian and foreign musicals and is one of the loveliest theaters in Moscow. Music lovers will not want to miss the Chaykovsky Concert Hall (**Концертный зал имени Чайковского** *kanTSERTny ZAL Imini chayKOFskava*). Visitors to St. Petersburg will surely want to see a performance at the Kirov Theater (**Театр имени Кирова** *tiATR Imini KIrava*) or the Maly Theater (**Малый театр** *MAly tiATR*).

Other special events in Moscow are the world famous Circus (**Цирк** *TSYRK*), sporting events, including spectacular hockey and soccer matches, the Russian version of the ice-capades (**Балет на льду** *baLYET na L'DU*), and song-and-dance ensembles, including the Red Army Chorus, Beriozka, the Pyatnitsky Choir, and individual artists. Ask your friends, hosts, and hotel personnel for their recommendations.

I would like to see ___ .	**Я хотел бы смотреть ___ .** *YA khaTYEL BY smaTRYET'*
■ a ballet	**балет** *baLYET*

▪ the circus	**цирк**	*TSYRK*
▪ a concert	**концерт**	*kanTSERT*
▪ a hockey match	**хоккей**	*khaKYEY*
▪ a movie	**фильм**	*FIL'M*
▪ an opera	**оперу**	*Opiru*
▪ a soccer match	**футбол**	*fudBOL*

What is playing?	**Что идёт?**	*SHTO iDYOT*
Who is playing?	**Кто играет?**	*KTO iGRAyit*
Is it an opera or a ballet?	**Это опера или балет?**	*Eta Opira Ili baLYET*
I like ____ .	**Я люблю ____ .**	*YA lyuBLYU*
▪ classical music	**классическую музыку**	*klaSIchiskuyu MUzyku*
▪ modern music	**современную музыку**	*savriMYEnuyu MUzyku*
▪ folk music	**народную музыку**	*naRODnuyu MUzyku*
What kind of film is it?	**Что это за фильм?**	*SHTO Eta za FIL'M*

A comedy?	**Комедия?** *kaMYEdiya*
A drama?	**Трагедия?** *traGYEdiya*
A love story?	**Любовная история?** *lyuBOVnaya iSTOriya*
A musical?	**Музыкальный фильм?** *muzyKAL'ny FIL'M*
A mystery film?	**Детектив?** *ditikTIF*
A science fiction film?	**Научно–популярный фильм?** *naUCHna-papuLYARny FIL'M*
A war film?	**Фильм о войне?** *FIL'M a vayNYE*
Are there seats for tonight's performance?	**Есть билеты на сегодня вечером?** *YEST' biLYEty na siVODnya VYEchiram*
What kind of seats do you have?	**Какие у вас места?** *kaKIye u VAS miSTA*
One orchestra seat please.	**Один в партере, пожалуйста.** *aDIN f parTYErye paZHAlusta*
Two balcony seats.	**Два в балконе.** *DVA v balKOnye*
Three in the first ring.	**Три в первом ярусе.** *TRI f PYERvam YArusye*
What are the least expensive seats?	**Какие самые дешёвые места?** *kaKIye SAmiye diSHOviye miSTA*
When does the performance begin?	**Когда спектакль начинается?** *kagDA spikTAKL' nachiNAyitsa*
When is the performance over?	**Когда спектакль кончается?** *kagDA spikTAKL' kanCHAyitsa*
Who has an extra ticket?	**У кого лишний билет?** *u kaVO LISHny biLYET*
Are they letting people in?	**Уже пускают?** *uZHE pusKAyut*
Please go in.	**Проходите, пожалуйста.** *prakhaDItye paZHAlusta*

When you arrive at the theater you should show your ticket, then proceed to the coat check racks (**Гардероб** *gardiROP*). You must leave your coat and hat, and you may leave your briefcase or packages. Many women change from boots into more comfortable and attractive shoes. There is no charge for cloakroom service, but a modest fee is charged for rental of opera glasses. The few rubles that the attendants earn this way substitute for tips. In addition, custom permits those returning opera glasses to go to the head of the line after the performance.

Opera glasses, please.	**Бинокль, пожалуйста.**	*biNOKL' paZHAlusta*
I'll take a program.	**Я возьму программку.**	*YA vaz'MU praGRAMku*
Where are our seats?	**Где наши места?**	*GDYE NAshi miSTA*
Who is the conductor?	**Кто дирижёр?**	*KTO diriZHOR*
Who's singing?	**Кто поёт?**	*KTO paYOT*
Who's dancing?	**Кто танцует?**	*KTO tanTSUyit*
Will there be an intermission?	**Будет антракт?**	*BUdit anTRAKT*

YOUR TICKET

Your theater ticket will contain much valuable information. Examine it carefully. On the front will be printed the name and symbol of your theater, the starting time of the performance, the location of your seats, including row and seat number, and the date of the performance. The back of the ticket will give the title of the performance and may provide information on public transportation to the theater.

Главное управление культуры исполкома Моссовета
Московский академический ордена Трудового Красного Знамени музыкальный театр
Пушкинская ул., 17   Тел. 229-28-35
Серия НН ВЕЧЕР Начало в 19 часов
БЕЛЬЭТАЖ
000518   **РЯД 8   МЕСТО 33**
1 ДЕК 1989   **Цена 90 коп.**
КОНТРОЛЬ
МУЗЫКАЛЬНЫЙ ТЕАТР

The theater	**Большой Театр** *Bolshoi*
	Кремлёвский Дворец съездов *Palace of Congress*
	Малый Театр *Maly*
	Музыкальный Театр *Stanislavsky Musical*
Starting time	**Начало в 12 часов** *Noon*
	Начало в 19 часов *7:00* PM
	Начало в 20 часов *8:00* PM
Location	**Партер** *Orchestra*
	Амфитеатр *Rear Orchestra*
	Бельэтаж *Mezzanine*
	Балкон *Balcony*
	Ложа *Box*
	1 Ярус *First Ring*
	Правая сторона *Right*
	Левая сторона *Left*
	Середина *Center*
	Ряд *Row*
	Место *Seat*
	Цена 1 рубль *Price*

NIGHTCLUBS

For late evening entertainment, try one of the nightclubs or restaurants with floor shows. In Moscow late shows are also presented at the hotels Intourist, Kosmos, and International (**Международная** *mizhdunaRODnaya*) and at the restaurant Arbat.

Let's go to a nightclub. **Пойдём в ночной бар.** *payDYOM v nachNOY BAR*

Are reservations necessary?	**Надо заказать заранее?** *NAda zakaZAT' zaRAniye*
I feel like dancing.	**Мне хочется танцевать.** *MNYE KHOchitsa tantsiVAT'*
Is there a discotheque here?	**Здесь есть дискотека?** *ZDYES' YEST' diskaTYEka*
What is the cover charge?	**Сколько стоит входной билет?** *SKOL'ka STOit fkhadNOY biLYET*
A table close to the stage.	**Столик поближе к сцене.** *STOlik paBLIzhe k TSEnye*
When does the show begin?	**Когда варьете начинается?** *kagDA var'yiTYE nachiNAyitsa*

QUIET RELAXATION: CARDS, CHESS

Do you have a deck of cards?	**Нет ли у вас колода карт?** *NYET LI u VAS kaLOda KART*
Would you like to play cards?	**Не хотите играть в карты?** *NYE khaTItye iGRAT' f KARty*
Do you want to shuffle?	**Перетасуете?** *piriTAsuyitye*
Cut the deck!	**Снимите!** *sniMItye*
hearts, diamonds, clubs, spades	**черви, бубны, трефы, пики** *CHERvi, BUBny, TRYEfy, PIki,*
ace, king, queen, jack	**туз, король, дама, валет** *TUS, kaROL', DAma, vaLYET*
Whose turn is it?	**Кому ходить?** *kaMU khaDIT'*
It's your deal.	**Вам сдавать.** *VAM zdaVAT'*
What's the score?	**Какой счёт?** *kaKOY SHOT*
You win.	**Вы выиграли.** *VY VYigrali*
I lose.	**Я проиграл.** *YA praiGRAL*

Do you want to play ____ ?	**Хотите играть ____ ?**	*khaTItye iGRAT'*
checkers	**в шашки**	*f SHASHki*
chess	**в шахматы**	*f SHAKHmaty*
We need a board.	**Нам нужна доска.**	*NAM nuzhNA daSKA*
We need the pieces.	**Нам нужны фигуры.**	*NAM nuzhNY fiGUry*
the king	**король**	*kaROL'*
the queen	**королева**	*karaLYEva*
the rook	**ладья**	*laD'YA*
the bishop	**слон**	*SLON*
the knight	**офицер**	*ofiTSER*
the pawn	**пешка**	*PYESHka*
Check.	**Шах.**	*SHAKH*
Checkmate.	**Мат.**	*MAT*

SPORTS

In addition to watching the popular spectator sports, Russians love to spend time outdoors. You might spend the afternoon in one of the major parks or go swimming in one of the outdoor pools open all year. Winter sports include skating, sledding, and cross country skiing near Lenin Hills. You can also play tennis, and a golf course recently opened near Moscow.

BEACH or POOL

Oh! It's hot!	**Ой! Как жарко!**	*OY KAK ZHARka*
Let's go swimming.	**Пойдём купаться.**	*payDYOM kuPAtsa*
Let's go to the beach.	**Пойдём на пляж.**	*payDYOM na PLYASH*
Let's go to the pool.	**Пойдём в бассейн.**	*payDYOM v baSYEYN*

How do you get there?	**Как туда проехать?** *KAK tuDA praYEkhat'*
What's the admission charge?	**Сколько стоит билет?** *SKOL'ka STOit biLYET*
What's the water temperature?	**Сколько градусов воды?** *SKOL'ka GRAdusaf vaDY*
I (don't) know how to swim.	**Я (не) умею плавать.** *YA (NYE) uMYEyu PLAvat'*
Is there a lifeguard?	**Есть спасатель?** *YEST spaSAtil'*
Where is the locker room?	**Где камера хранения?** *GDYE KAmira khraNYEniya*
Can I rent ____ ?	**Можно взять на прокат ____ ?** *MOZHna VZYAT' na praKAT*
▣ an air mattress	**надувной матрац** *naduvNOY maTRATS*
▣ a beach ball	**мяч** *MYACH*
▣ a boat	**лодку** *LOTku*
▣ a chaise longue	**шезлонг** *shizLONG*
▣ a beach towel	**полотенце** *palaTYENtse*
▣ an umbrella	**зонт** *ZONT*
▣ water skis	**водные лыжи** *vadNIye LYzhi*
I need to buy ____ .	**Мне надо купить ____ .** *MNYE NAda kuPIT'*
▣ a bathing cap	**шапочку** *SHApachku*
▣ a bathing suit	**купальник** *kuPAL'nik*
▣ bathing trunks	**плавки** *PLAFki*
▣ sunglasses	**солнечные очки** *SOL'nichniye achKI*
▣ suntan lotion	**крем от загара** *KRYEM at zaGAra*

WINTER SPORTS

I want to go ____ .	**Я хочу кататься ____ .** *YA khaCHU kaTAtsa*
▣ ice skating	**на коньках** *na kan'KAKH*

▨ skiing	**на лыжах**	*na LYzhakh*
▨ sledding	**на санках**	*na SANkakh*
Where can I buy ____ ?	**Где купить ____ ?**	*GDYE kuPIT'*
▨ bindings	**крепления**	*kriPLYEniya*
▨ boots	**ботинки/сапоги**	*baTINki/sapaGI*
▨ cross country skis	**беговые лыжи**	*bigaVIye LYzhi*
▨ down hill skis	**горные лыжи**	*GORniye LYzhi*
▨ poles	**палки**	*PALki*
▨ figure skates	**фигурные коньки**	*fiGURniye kan'KI*
▨ hockey skates	**хоккейные коньки**	*khaKYEYniye kan'KI*

IN THE COUNTRYSIDE

Let's go to the country.	**Поедем в деревню.**	*paYEdim v diRYEVnyu*

Do you have a dacha in the country?	**У вас есть дача в деревне?** *u VAS YEST' DAcha v diRYEVnye*
How long does it take to get there?	**Сколько времени туда ехать?** *SKOL'ka VRYEmini tuDA YEkhat'*
How beautiful!	**Как красиво!** *KAK kraSIva*
Look at the _____ .	**Посмотрите на _____ .** *pasmaTRItye na*
🔲 birds	**птиц** *PTITS*
🔲 bridge	**мост** *MOST*
🔲 brook	**ручей** *ruCHYEY*
🔲 fields	**поля** *paLYA*
🔲 flowers	**цветы** *tsviTY*
🔲 forest	**лес** *LYES*
🔲 hills	**холмы** *khalMY*
🔲 lake	**озеро** *Ozira*
🔲 mountains	**горы** *GOry*
🔲 plants	**растения** *raSTYEniya*
🔲 pond	**пруд** *PRUT*
🔲 river	**реку** *RYEku*
🔲 sea	**море** *MOrye*
🔲 trees	**деревья** *diRYEv'ya*
🔲 village	**село** *siLO*
🔲 valley	**долину** *daLInu*
I'm lost.	**Я потерялся.** *YA patiRYALsya*
Where does _____ lead?	**Куда идёт _____ ?** *kuDA iDYOT*
🔲 this road	**эта дорога** *Eta daROga*
🔲 this path	**эта тропинка** *Eta traPINka*
Can you show me the way?	**Вы можете мне показать дорогу?** *VY MOzhitye MNYE pakaZAT' daROgu*

FOOD AND DRINK

A restaurant meal in Russia is an event to be enjoyed and savored for the better part of an evening. For a quick bite to eat, visit one of the local **Пельменная**   *pil'MYEnaya* (Siberian dumpling), **Шашлычная**   *shaSHLYCHnaya* (shish-kabob), or **Гриль**   *GRIL'* (grill) establishments. When during out you will have the choice not only of Russian cuisine, but also of exceptional national cuisines such as Armenian, Georgian, and Uzbek. The Russian breakfast tends to be simple, but hearty. You might have a pastry or the famous Russian dark bread with butter and marmalade. You can also have **каша**   *KAsha* (a warm cereal), **сосиски**   *saSISki* (hot dogs), or **яйца**   *YAYtsa* (eggs), accompanied by a glass of **русский чай**   *RUski CHAY* (Russian tea) with plenty of **сахар**   *SAkhar* (sugar). Because lunch tends to be the main meal of the day, Russians typically will have a **салат**   *saLAT* (salad), **суп**   *SUP* (soup), a main course, and a light dessert, accompanied by more **чёрный хлеб**   *CHORny KHLYEP* (black bread). An excellent selection for lunch is offered at the major hotels, which often feature a smorgasbord (**Шведский стол**   *SHVYETski STOL*) for lunch at reasonable prices. Thus, you can sample a variety of dishes. In the evening you might have a light snack of **бутерброды**   *butirBROdy* (open-faced sandwiches), with **икра**   *iKRA* (caviar), **сыр**   *SYR* (cheese), **рыба**   *RYba* (fish) or **мясо**   *MYAsa* (meat), and a **пирожное**   *piROZHnaye* (sweet pastry) at one of the theater buffets. If you go to a restaurant, there will likely be elaborate **закуски**   *zaKUSki* (hors d'œuvres) including assorted meats, fish, patés, and cucumbers and tomatoes with sour cream, with ample amounts of vodka, wine, or champagne for the numerous toasts normally accompanying such a feast. Through Intourservice you may order a full seven-course meal with a set menu at one of Moscow's or St. Petersburg's famous restaurants. To go on your own, make reservations in person for that evening at a restaurant.

A recent addition to the restaurant scene is dozens of cooperative ventures (**кооперативы**   *kaapiraTIvy*). Although these tend to be considerably more expensive, they provide excellent service and delicious food and offer a lovely atmosphere for a special evening. Many of them accept hard currency and credit cards. You should determine the means of payment when you make a reservation, which is an absolute must at most cooperatives.

EATING OUT

The main Russian meals are

breakfast	**завтрак**	*ZAFtrak*
lunch	**обед**	*aBYET*
supper	**ужин**	*Uzhin*

You will probably come across the following establishments serving food.

buffet	**буфет**	*buFYET*
cafe	**кафе**	*kaFYEY*
cafeteria	**столовая**	*staLOvaya*
grill	**гриль**	*GRIL'*
ice cream parlor	**кафе мороженое**	*kaFYEY maROzhinaye*
pancake house	**блинная**	*BLInaya*
pelmennaya (Siberian dumpling shop)	**пельменная**	*pil'MYEnaya*
restaurant	**ресторан**	*ristaRAN*
shashlychnaya (shish-kabob)	**шашлычная**	*shaSHLYCHnaya*
snack bar	**закусочная**	*zaKUsachnaya*

Do you know a good restaurant?	**Вы знаете хороший ресторан?** *VY ZNAyitye khaROshi ristaRAN*
Is it very expensive?	**Он очень дорогой?** *ON Ochin' daraGOY*
Can I sample Russian cuisine there?	**Там можно попробовать русскую кухню?** *TAM MOZHna paPRObavat' RUskuyu KUKHnyu*
I'd like to reserve a table _____ .	**Я хочу заказать стол _____ .** *YA khaCHU zakaZAT' STOL*
▮ for tonight	**на сегодня** *na siVODnya*

■ for tomorrow evening   **на завтра**   *na ZAFtra*

■ for two (three, four) persons   **на двоих (троих, четверых)**   *na dvaIKH (traIKH, chitviRYKH)*

■ at 8:00 PM (20:00)   **в двадцать часов**   *v DVAtsat' chiSOF*

Waiter!   **Молодой человек!**   *malaDOY chilaVYEK*

Miss!   **Девушка!**   *DYEvushka*

The customs surrounding a Russian restaurant meal deserve a minute of your attention. You should be attentive to signs posted on the front door. **Перерыв** *piriRYF* indicates that the restaurant is closed for a break between meals. **Свободных мест нет** *svaBODnykh MYEST NYET* means no free places at the moment. You might want to wait, but in the evening most Russians will stay until closing time. When you get past the doorman, check your coat and hat at the **Гардероб** *gardiROP*. From there you proceed to the *maitre d' hotel* (**метрдотель** *mitrdaTYEL'*), who will escort you to a table. Unless your party is large enough to fill an entire table, strangers may be seated next to you. If you are alone, there will be a wait until all the seats at the table are occupied; thus it is in your interest to pick a place at a partially occupied table that has not yet been served. When the waiter (**официант** *afitsiANT*) or waitress (**официантка** *afitsiANTka*) approaches, you will hear "**Я вас слушаю** *YA VAS SLUshayu*"; literally, "I am listening," which means "I am ready to take your order." Normally you will order the entire meal at that time, including dessert (**сладкое** *SLATkaye*) and coffee or tea.

Is this table being served?   **Этот стол обслуживается?**   *Etat STOL apSLUzhivayitsa*

Please bring the menu.   **Меню, пожалуйста.**   *miNYU paZHAlusta*

What is your specialty?	**Какое у вас фирменное блюдо?** *kaKOye u VAS FIRminaye BLYUda*
I'm (not) very hungry. (*m*)	**Я (не) очень голоден.** *YA (NYE) Ochin' GOladin*
I'm (not) very hungry. (*f*)	**Я (не) очень голодна.** *YA (NYE) Ochin' galadNA*
To begin with, bring us ____ .	**Для начала, принесите нам ____ .** *dlya naCHAla priniSItye NAM*
▪ some vodka (100 grams)	**сто грамм водки** *STO GRAM VOTki*
▪ some cognac (100 grams)	**сто грамм коньяка** *STO GRAM kan'yaKA*
▪ a bottle of red wine	**бутылку красного вина** *buTYLku KRASnava viNA*
▪ a bottle of white wine	**бутылку белого вина** *buTYLku BYElava viNA*
▪ a bottle of beer	**бутылку пива** *buTYLku PIva*
▪ a bottle of mineral water	**бутылку минеральной воды** *buTYLku miniRAL'nay vaDY*
▪ a bottle of soft drink	**бутылку лимонада** *buTYLku limaNAda*
I'm ready to order now.	**Я готов заказать.** *YA gaTOF zakaZAT'*
What do you recommend?	**Что вы рекомендуете?** *SHTO VY rikaminDUyitye*
Please also bring us ____ .	**Принесите, пожалуйста ____ .** *priniSItye paZHAlusta*
▪ some bread	**хлеба** *KHLYEba*
▪ some butter	**масла** *MAsla*
▪ some more ____	**ещё ____** *yiSHO*
▪ an ashtray	**пепельницу** *PYEpil'nitsu*
▪ a knife	**нож** *NOSH*
▪ a fork	**вилку** *VILku*

a spoon	**ложку**	*LOSHku*
a glass	**стакан**	*staKAN*
a vodka glass	**рюмку**	*RYUMku*
a plate	**тарелку**	*taRYELku*
a napkin	**салфетку**	*salFYETku*
I'll have the _____ .	**Я возьму** _____ .	*YA vaz'MU*

THE MENU

Russian menus are pre-printed and are often several pages long. Only those selections with a price indicated are available. Even so, you might ask whether your favorite dish can be ordered.

APPETIZERS (ЗАКУСКИ)
COLD (ХОЛОДНЫЕ) and WARM (ЖАРКИЕ)

At banquets and formal dinners great care, attention, and expense are devoted to appetizers (**закуски** *zaKUSki*), which accompany the obligatory toasts with Russian vodka. It is important to dig in and help yourself. Russians recommend black bread spread with lots of butter and cucumbers sprinkled with salt as a way to compensate for the alcohol. You will be delighted by the variety of items, which can range from elaborate fish trays to exquisite caviar. But if you are on a tight budget, be sure to ask in advance what all this costs.

assorted fish	**ассорти рыбное**	*asarTI RYBnaye*
assorted meats	**ассорти мясное**	*asarTI misNOye*
caviar	**икра**	*iKRA*
black caviar	**зернистая икра**	*zirNIStaya iKRA*
red caviar	**кетовая икра**	*KYEtavaya iKRA*
mushrooms	**грибы**	*griBY*
mushrooms julienne	**жульен из грибов**	*zhuL'YEN iz griBOF*
sandwich	**бутерброд**	*butirBROT*

EGGS (ЯЙЦО)

hard-boiled eggs	**яйца вкрутую**	*YAYtsa fkruTUyu*
soft-boiled eggs	**яйца всмятку**	*YAYtsa FSMYATku*
fried eggs	**яичница-глазунья**	*yaICHnitsa glaZUn'ya*
scrambled eggs	**яичница-болтунья**	*yaICHnitsa balTUn'ya*

SALADS (САЛАТ)

In addition to the standard salad dishes, almost every restaurant has its house specialty salad (**салат** *saLAT*). Ask the waiter about the ingredients, and wait to be pleasantly surprised, visually and gastronomically.

crab salad	**салат из крабов**	*saLAT is KRAbaf*
tomato salad	**салат из помидиров**	*saLAT is pamiDOraf*
cucumber salad	**салат из огурцов**	*saLAT iz agurTSOF*

SOUPS (СУП)
THE FIRST COURSE (ПЕРВОЕ)

Soup (**суп** *SUP*) is an absolute must in the winter, but even in the summer months Russians enjoy their soups. The most frequently encountered soups are **борщ** *BORSH* made of beets, **щи** *SHI*, made from cabbage, or **солянка** *saIYANka*, made from fish or meat.

beet soup	**борщ**	*BORSH*
bouillon	**бульон**	*buL'YON*
cabbage soup	**щи**	*SHI*
fish soup	**рыбный суп**	*RYBny SUP*
kidney soup	**рассольник**	*raSOL'nik*
mushroom soup	**грибной суп**	*gribNOY SUP*
noodle soup	**суп-лапша**	*SUP-lapSHA*
solyanka	**солянка**	*saLYANka*

THE MAIN (SECOND) COURSE (ВТОРОЕ)

For the main course, much will depend upon the availability of different fish (**рыба** *RYba*) and meat (**мясо** *MYAsa*) dishes. Here too, you might inquire about the **фирменные блюда** *FIRminiye BLYUda* (house specialties).

FISH (РЫБА)

carp	**карп** *KARP*
cod	**треска** *triSKA*
herring	**селёдка** *siLYOTka*
pike perch	**судак** *suDAK*
salmon	**сёмга** *SYOMga*
sturgeon	**осетрина** *asiTRIna*
filet of sturgeon	**балык** *baLYK*
trout	**форель** *faRYEL'*

MEAT (МЯСО)

beef Stroganoff	**беф-строганов** *bif-STROganaf*
steak	**бифштекс** *bifSHTYEKS*
cutlets	**котлеты** *katLYEty*
golubtsy (stuffed cabbage)	**голубцы** *galupTSY*
roast beef	**ростбиф** *ROSTbif*
lamb	**баранина** *baRAnina*
liver	**печень** *PYEchin'*
pelmeni (Siberian dumplings)	**пельмени** *pil'MYEni*
pork chops	**свиные отбивные котлеты** *sviNIye atbivNIye katLYEty*
ragout	**рагу** *raGU*
Schnitzel	**шницель** *SHNItsil'*

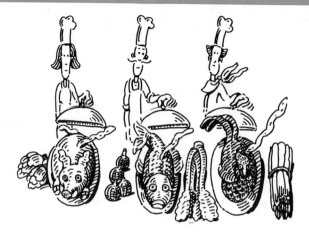

veal	**телятина** *tiLYAtina*
fried	**жареный** *ZHAriny*
grilled	**обжаренный** *abZHAriny*
baked	**печёный** *piCHOny*
boiled	**варёный** *vaRYOny*
stewed	**тушёный** *tuSHOny*

POULTRY (ПТИЦА)

chicken	**курица / цыплёнок** *KUritsa / tsyPLYOnak*
duck	**утка** *UTka*
goose	**гусь** *GUS'*
pheasant	**фасан** *faSAN*
poultry	**птица** *PTItsa*
turkey	**индейка** *inDYEYka*

DESSERTS (СЛАДКОЕ)
THE THIRD COURSE (ТРЕТЬЕ)

stewed fruit	компот	*kamPOT*
ice cream	мороженое	*maROzhinaye*
fresh fruits	свежие фрукты	*SVYEzhiye FRUKty*
whipped cream	взбитые сливки	*VZBItiye SLIFki*

BEVERAGES (НАПИТКИ)

A word should be said about beverages (**напитки** *naPITki*), especially alcoholic ones. In recent years the Russian government has taken steps to ensure that alcoholic consumption stays within reasonable bounds. Officially, the amount of vodka or cognac that can be ordered in a restaurant is limited and carefully monitored. Cooperative restaurants do not have liquor licenses. Nonetheless, you are likely to be entertained at a number of events where vodka, cognac, wine, and champagne are available in liberal quantities. Drinking for Russians is surrounded with ceremony, including the obligation for the host to raise a toast, after which most Russians empty their glasses by drinking **до дна** *da DNA* (bottoms up, literally "to the bottom"). You should not feel compelled after the first toast to keep pace with your hosts. Remember to eat something for every glass and to follow the lead of the Russians and drink liberal amounts of **минеральная вода** *miniRAL'naya vaDA* (mineral water) between toasts.

beer	пиво	*PIva*
champagne	шампанское	*shamPANskaye*
■ very dry	сухое	*suKHOye*
■ semi-dry	полусухое	*palusuKHOye*
■ sweet	сладкое	*SLATkaye*
cognac	коньяк	*kaN'YAK*
coffee	кофе	*KOfye*
■ with milk	с молоком	*s malaKOM*
_____ juice	_____ сок	*SOK*
■ apple	яблочный	*YAblachny*

	grape	**виноградный** *vinaGRADny*
▨	orange	**апельсиновый** *apil'SInavy*
	kvass	**квас** *KVAS*
	milk	**молоко** *malaKO*
	mineral water	**минеральная вода** *miniRAL'naya vaDA*
	soft drink	**лимонад** *limaNAT*
	tea	**чай** *CHAY*
▨	with lemon	**с лимоном** *s liMOnam*
▨	with sugar	**с сахаром** *s SAkharam*
	——— wine	**——— вино** *viNO*
▨	Armenian	**армянское** *arMYANskaye*
▨	Georgian	**грузинское** *gruZINskaye*
▨	dry	**сухое** *suKHOye*
▨	red	**красное** *KRASnaye*
▨	sweet	**сладкое** *SLATkaye*
▨	white	**белое** *BYElaye*

SETTLING UP

Your bill probably will include a ten-percent service charge. You might choose to leave your small change as a token of your satisfaction with the service.

The check, please.	**Счёт, пожалуйста.** *SHOT paZHAlusta*
Separate checks, please.	**Посчитайте отдельно, пожалуйста.** *pashiTAYtye aDYEL'na paZHAlusta*
Is service included?	**Обслуживание входит в счёт?** *apSLUzhivaniye FKHOdit f SHOT*
I didn't order this.	**Я этого не заказывал.** *YA Etava NYE zaKAzyval*

Please check the bill.	**Проверьте счёт, пожалуйста.** *praVYER'tye SHOT paZHAlusta*
It appears you've made an error.	**Кажется, что вы ошиблись.** *KAzhitsa SHTO VY aSHYblis'*
We are in a hurry.	**Мы спешим.** *MY spiSHYM*
Will it take long?	**Нам долго ждать?** *NAM DOLga ZHDAT'*
This is for you.	**Это для вас.** *Eta dlya VAS*

SHOPPING FOR FOOD

Sometime during your stay you'll probably want to purchase something for a midnight snack or an early morning start. You might visit a bakery (**булочная** *BUlachnaya*) or a pastry shop (**кондитерская** *kanDItirskaya*), try out a Russian style supermarket (**гастроном** *gastraNOM*), or buy something at an outdoor market (**рынок** *RYnak*) or the stands on the streetcorners. Most items are sold by weight, and you'll purchase many things by the hundred grams (about one quarter of a pound) or by the kilogram (two and one quarter American pounds).

BREADS (ХЛЕБ)
THE BAKERY (БУЛОЧНАЯ)

a loaf of white bread	**батон белого хлеба** *baTON BYElava KHLYEba*
dark bread	**чёрный хлеб** *CHORny KHLYEP*
rye bread	**ржаной хлеб** *rzhaNOY KHLYEP*
a roll	**булочка** *BUlachka*

DAIRY PRODUCTS
MILK and CHEESE (МОЛОКО и СЫР)

Russian cheese	**российский сыр** *raSIYski SYR*
Dutch cheese	**голландский сыр** *gaLANTski SYR*

creamy butter	**сливочное масло** *SLIvachnaye MAsla*
chocolate butter	**шоколадное масло** *shakaLADnaye MAsla*
cream cheese	**творог** *tvaROK*
sour cream	**сметана** *smiTAna*
kefir (a yogurt-like beverage)	**кефир** *kiFIR*

CAKES (ТОРТЫ)
THE PASTRY SHOP (КОНДИТЕРСКАЯ)

jelly	**варенье** *vaRYEn'ye*
muffins/cupcakes	**кекс** *KYEKS*
a round cookie	**кольцо** *kal'TSO*
oatmeal cookies	**овсянное печенье** *afSYAnaye piCHEn'ye*
a cake	**торт** *TORT*
a pie	**пирог** *piROK*
pastry	**пирожное** *piROZHnaye*

SEASONINGS (ПРИПРАВА)

saccharin	**сахарин** *sakhaRIN*
sugar	**сахар** *SAkhar*
salt	**соль** *SOL'*
pepper	**перец** *PYErits*
horseradish	**хрен** *KHRYEN*
mayonnaise	**майонез** *mayaNYES*
mustard	**горчица** *garCHItsa*
garlic	**чеснок** *chiSNOK*
vegetable oil	**растительное масло** *raSTItil'naye MAsla*
vinegar	**уксус** *UKsus*

COLD CUTS

ham	**ветчина**	*vichiNA*
salami	**колбаса**	*kalbaSA*

FRUITS (ФРУКТЫ)

apple	**яблоко**	*YAblaka*
apricot	**абрикос**	*abriKOS*
banana	**банан**	*baNAN*
cherry	**вишня**	*VISHnya*
currants	**смородина**	*smaROdina*
date	**финик**	*FInik*
fig	**фига**	*FIga*
grapefruit	**грейпфрут**	*GRYEYPfrut*
grapes	**виноград**	*vinaGRAT*
lemon	**лимон**	*liMON*
melon	**дыня**	*DYnya*
orange	**апельсин**	*apil'SIN*
pear	**груша**	*GRUsha*
peach	**персик**	*PYERsik*
pineapple	**ананас**	*anaNAS*
plum	**слива**	*SLIva*
pomegranate	**гранат**	*graNAT*
raspberries	**малина**	*maLIna*
strawberries	**клубник**	*klubNIK*
tangerine	**мандарин**	*mandaRIN*
watermelon	**арбуз**	*arBUS*
almonds	**миндаль**	*minDAL'*
chestnuts	**каштан**	*kaSHTAN*
nuts	**орехи**	*aRYEkhi*

ICE CREAM (МОРОЖЕНОЕ)

_____ ice cream	_____ **мороженое** *maROzhinaye*
◼ chocolate	**шоколадное** *shakaLADnaye*
◼ vanilla	**сливочное** *SLIvachnaye*

VEGETABLES (ОВОЩИ)

asparagus	**спаржа** *SPARzha*
beets	**свёкла** *SVYOkla*
cabbage	**капуста** *kaPUSta*
carrots	**морковь** *marKOF'*
cauliflower	**цветная капуста** *tsvitNAya kaPUSta*
cucumbers	**огурцы** *agurTSY*
eggplant	**баклажан** *baklaZHAN*
lettuce	**салат** *saLAT*
mushrooms	**грибы** *griBY*
noodles	**лапша** *lapSHA*
onions	**лук** *LUK*
potatoes	**картофель** *karTOfil'*
pumpkin	**тыква** *TYKva*
radishes	**редиска** *riDISka*
rice	**рис** *RIS*
sauerkraut	**квашенная капуста** *KVAshinaya kaPUSta*
spinach	**шпинат** *shpiNAT*
string beans	**стручковая фасоль** *struchKOvaya faSOL'*
tomatoes	**помидоры** *pamiDOry*
turnips	**репька** *RYEP'ka*

MEETING PEOPLE

GREETINGS AND INTRODUCTIONS

Hello!	**Здравствуйте!** *ZDRASTvuytye*
My name is ___ .	**Меня зовут** ___ . *miNYA zaVUT*
What is your name?	**Как вас зовут?** *KAK VAS zaVUT*

> Russians use three names, a first name **имя** *Imya*, a patronymic derived from one's father's name **отчество** *Ochistva*, and a family name **фамилия** *faMIliya*. It is polite to refer to recent acquaintances with the name and patronymic. Thus one would address even Mr. Gorbachev as **Михаил Сергеевич** *mikhaIL sirGYEyivich*. Russians are likely to have a nickname. For example, Ivan—**Иван** *iVAN* becomes Vanya—**Ваня** *VAnya*, Aleksandr—**Александр** *alikSANDR* becomes Sasha—**Саша** *SAsha*.

Pleased to meet you.	**Очень приятно.** *Ochin' priYATna*
I am from ___ .	**Я из** ___ . *YA iz*
▪ Australia	**Австралии** *afSTRAlii*
▪ Canada	**Канады** *kaNAdy*
▪ England	**Англии** *ANglii*
▪ the USA	**США** *SA SHA A*
I like ___ very much.	**Мне очень нравится** ___ . *MNYE Ochin' NRAvitsa*
▪ Moscow	**Москва** *maskVA*
▪ Leningrad	**Ленинград** *lininGRAT*
▪ your country	**ваша страна** *VAsha straNA*
▪ your republic	**ваша республика** *VAsha riSPUblika*

May I introduce myself.	**Разрешите мне представиться.**
	razriSHYtye MNYE pritSTAvitsa
May I introduce my _____ .	**Разрешите мне представить _____ .**
	razriSHYtye MNYE pritSTAvit'
brother	**брата** *BRAta*
colleague	**коллегу** *kaLYEgu*
daughter	**дочь** *DOCH*
father	**отца** *aTSA*
friend	**друга** *DRUga*
husband	**мужа** *MUzha*
mother	**мать** *MAT'*
sister	**сестру** *siSTRU*
wife	**жену** *zhiNU*
son	**сына** *SYna*

I am ____ .	**Я ____ .** *YA*
an artist	**художник** *khuDOZHnik*
a builder	**строитель** *straItel'*
a businessman	**бизнесмен** *biznisMYEN*
a correspondent	**корреспондент** *karispanDYENT*
a diplomat	**дипломат** *diplaMAT*
a doctor	**врач** *VRACH*
a dentist	**зубной врач** *zubNOY VRACH*
a lawyer	**адвокат** *advaKAT*
a teacher	**преподаватель** *pripadaVAtil'*
a student	**студент** *stuDYENT*
a nurse	**медсестра** *medsiSTRA*
a writer	**писатель** *piSAtil'*
Where are you from?	**Откуда вы?** *atKUda VY*
Where do you work?	**Где вы работаете?** *GDYE VY raBOtayitye*
What is your profession?	**Кто вы по профессии?** *KTO VY papraFYEsii*
I will be staying ____ .	**Я здесь буду ____ .** *YA ZDYES' BUdu*
a few days	**несколько дней** *NYEskal'ka DNYEY*
a week	**неделю** *niDYElyu*
a month	**месяц** *MYEsits*
Would you like a picture?	**Хотите фотографию?** *khaTItye fataGRAfiyu*
Stand there.	**Стойте там.** *STOYtye TAM*
Smile!	**Улыбайтесь!** *ulyBAYtis'*
Say "cheese"! ("raisin")	**Скажите "изюм"!** *skaZHYtye iZYUM*
I want a photo of you.	**Я хочу фотографию вас.** *YA khaCHU fataGRAfiyu VAS*
as a remembrance	**на память** *na PAmit'*

SOCIALIZING

May I have this dance? (May I invite you?)	**Разрешите вас пригласить?** *razriSHYtye VAS priglaSIT'*
All right. With pleasure.	**Хорошо. С удовольствием.** *kharaSHO s udaVOL'STviyim*
Would you like a cigarette?	**Закурите?** *zaKUritye*
Would you like a drink?	**Что-нибудь выпьете?** *SHTO-nibut' VYpitye*
Do you mind if I smoke?	**Ничего если я закурю?** *nichiVO YEsli YA zakuRYU*
May I take you home?	**Можно вас домой проводить?** *MOZHna VAS daMOY pravaDIT'*
May I call you?	**Можно вам позвонить?** *MOZHna VAM pazvaNIT'*
What is your telephone number?	**Какой ваш номер телефона?** *kaKOY VASH NOmir tiliFOna*
Here is my telephone number.	**Вот мой номер телефона.** *VOT MOY NOmir tiliFOna*
Here is my address.	**Вот мой адрес.** *VOT MOY Adris*
Will you write to me?	**Вы мне напишете?** *VY MNYE naPIshitye*
Are you married? (of a man)	**Вы женаты?** *VY zhiNAty*
Are you married? (of a woman)	**Вы замужем?** *VY ZAmuzhim*
Are you alone? (of a man)	**Вы один?** *VY aDIN*
Are you alone? (of a woman)	**Вы одна?** *VY adNA*
Is your husband here?	**Ваш муж здесь?** *VASH MUSH ZDYES'*
Is your wife here?	**Ваша жена здесь?** *VAsha zhiNA ZDYES'*

I'm here with my family.	**Я здесь с семьёй.** *YA ZDYES' s siM'YOY*
Do you have children?	**У вас есть дети?** *u VAS YEST' DYEti*
How many?	**Сколько?** *SKOL'ka*
How old are they?	**Сколько им лет?** *SKOL'ka IM LYET*
What are you doing tomorrow?	**Какие у вас планы на завтра?** *kaKIye u VAS PLAny na ZAFtra*
Are you free this evening?	**Вы свободны сегодня вечером?** *VY svaBODny siVODnya VYEchiram*
Would you like to go together?	**Хотите пойти вместе?** *khaTItye payTI VMYEStye*
I'll wait for you in front of the hotel.	**Я вас жду у входа гостиницы.** *YA VAS ZHDU u FKHOda gaSTInitsy*
I'll pick you up.	**Я за вами заеду.** *YA za VAmi zaYEdu*

SAYING GOODBYE

Thank you for your hospitality.	**Спасибо за гостеприимство.** *spaSIba za gastipriIMstva*
Nice to have met you.	**Очень приятно с вами познакомиться.** *Ochin' priYATna s VAmi paznaKOmitsa*
Regards to ____ .	**Привет ____ .** *priVYET*
Until tomorrow.	**До завтра.** *da ZAFtra*
Until later.	**Пока.** *paKA*
Until this evening.	**До вечера.** *da VYEchira*
Goodbye.	**До свидания.** *da sviDAniya*
Goodnight.	**Спокойной ночи.** *spaKOYnay NOchi*
Farewell.	**Прощайте.** *praSHAYtye*
I wish you ____ .	**Я желаю вам ____ .** *YA zhiLAyu VAM*
▓ all the best	**всего доброго** *fsiVO DObrava*
▓ bon voyage	**счастливого пути** *shastLIvava puTI*

SHOPPING

SHOPS AND STORES

To sample the wide variety of consumer items, you might begin with a visit to one of the large department stores in Moscow. Located on Red Square, the most famous store is GUM (**ГУМ**), the State Department Store. Just a few blocks away you can visit TSUM (**ЦУМ**), the Central Department Store, and Children's World (**Детский мир** *DYETski MIR*). There are also special stores for foreigners with access to freely convertible currencies (such as dollars, pounds, francs, and marks). These shops, called Beriozkas (**Берёзка** *biRYOSka*), often can be found in hotels. Russian stores open around 9:00 AM and remain open until about 8:00 PM. Many close for an hour during the lunch period. Signs posted on the door indicate the opening and closing times as well as the lunch break (**перерыв на обед** *piriRYF na aBYET*), but they will be listed according to the twenty-four hour clock. Thus 1:00 PM is 13:00 and 7:30 PM is 19:30. In addition to the stores you might try the farmers' market (**рынок** *RYnak*), the shopping mall along Arbat Street, and the Russian Fifth Avenue—Kalinin Prospekt. Many stores now offer goods produced by cooperatives—**кооперативные товары** *kaapiraTIVniye taVAry*. They are more expensive than standard items, but the workmanship tends to be superior.

GOING SHOPPING

I'd like to go shopping today.	**Сегодня я хочу пойти по магазинам.** *siVODnya YA khaCHUpayTI pa magaZInam.*
Where is a nearby _____ ?	**Где поблизости _____ ?** *GDYE paBLIzasti*
▪ antique shop	**комиссионный магазин** *kamisiOny magaZIN*
▪ bakery	**булочная** *BUlachnaya*

▣	barber shop	**парикмахерская** *parikMAkhirskaya*
▣	beauty parlor	**женский салон** *ZHENski saLON*
▣	bookstore	**книжный магазин** *KNIZHny magaZIN*
▣	butcher shop	**магазин "Мясо"** *magaZIN MYAsa*
▣	camera shop	**магазин "фототовары"** *magaZIN fotataVARY*
▣	candy store	**магазин "Конфеты"** *magaZIN kanFYEty*
▣	clothing store	**магазин "Одежда"** *magaZIN aDYEZHda*
▣	department store	**универмаг** *univirMAK*
▣	drugstore	**аптека** *apTYEka*
▣	dry cleaner's	**химчистка** *khimCHISTka*
▣	fabric store	**магазин "Ткани"** *magaZIN TKAni*
▣	florist	**магазин "Цветы"** *magaZIN tsviTY*
▣	fruit and vegetable store	**магазин "Овощи и Фрукты"** *magaZIN Ovashi I FRUKty*
▣	furrier	**магазин "Меха"** *magaZIN miKHA*
▣	gift (souvenir) store	**магазин "Подарки"** *magaZIN paDARki*
▣	hardware store	**хозяйственный магазин** *khaZYAYSTviny magaZIN*
▣	health-food store	**магазин "Диета"** *magaZIN diYEta*
▣	jewelry store	**ювелирный магазин** *yuviLIRny magaZIN*
▣	laundry	**прачечная** *PRAchichnaya*
▣	liquor store	**магазин "Вино"** *magaZIN viNO*
▣	newsstand	**газетный киоск** *gaZYETny kiOSK*
▣	optician	**оптика** *OPtika*
▣	pastry shop	**кондитерская** *kanDItirskaya*
▣	record store	**магазин "Пластинки"** *magaZIN plaSTINki*

▪ shoe store	**магазин "Обувь"**	*magaZIN Obuf'*
▪ shoe repair shop	**ремонт обуви**	*riMONT Obuvi*
▪ sporting goods store	**магазин "Спорттовары"**	*magaZIN sparttaVAry*
▪ stationery store	**канцелярские товары**	*kantsiLYARskiyetaVAry*
▪ supermarket	**гастроном**	*gastraNOM*
▪ tailor	**ателье мод**	*atiL'YE mot*
▪ tobacco shop	**магазин "Табак"**	*magaZIN taBAK*
▪ toiletries shop	**парфюмерия**	*parfyuMYEriya*
▪ toy store	**магазин "Игрушки"**	*magaZIN iGRUSHki*
▪ travel agent	**бюро путешествий**	*byuRO putiSHESTvi*
▪ watchmaker	**ремонт часов**	*riMONT chiSOF*
Young man!	**Молодой человек!**	*malaDOY chilaVYEK*
Young lady!	**Девушка!**	*DYEvushka*
Can you help me?	**Вы можете мне помочь _____ ?**	*VY MOzhitye MNYE paMOCH'*

In most Russian shops you first examine the articles
with the help of the salesperson behind the counter. When
you decide on your purchase, you need to find out the price.
Then you go to the cashier and tell him or her the total cost
and the department. After paying you receive a receipt
(**чек** *CHEK*), which you bring back to the original
counter, where your purchase will be waiting for you. If you
feel unsure of the Russian number system, you might have
the salesperson write down the price. The personnel are
scrupulously honest, and if you smile and show courtesy
and good humor you are likely to be helped through the
process.

BOOKS (КНИЖНЫЙ МАГАЗИН)

Where is the biggest (best) bookstore?	**Где самый большой (лучший) книжный магазин?** *GDYE SAmy bal'SHOY (LUCHshi) KNIZHny magaZIN*
How may I help you?	**Как вам помочь?** *KAK VAM paMOCH*
Go ahead! I'm listening.	**Говорите! Я вас слушаю.** *gavaRItye YA VAS SLUshayu*
Do you have books in English?	**У вас есть книги на английском языке?** *u VAS YEST' KNIgi na anGLIYskam yizyKYE*
The title of the book is ____ .	**Название книги ____ .** *naZVAniye KNIgi*
The author of the book is ____ .	**Автор книги ____ .** *AFtar KNIgi*
I don't know the title.	**Я не знаю названия.** *YA NYE ZNAyu naZVAniya*
I don't know the author.	**Я не знаю автора.** *YA NYE ZNAyu AFtara*
I'm just looking.	**Я только смотрю.** *YA TOL'ka smaTRYU*
I would like to buy ____ .	**Я хотел бы купить ____ .** *YA khaTYEL BY kuPIT'*
▪ a guide book	**путеводитель** *putivaDItil'*
▪ a map of this city	**план города** *PLAN GOrada*
▪ a pocket dictionary	**карманный словарь** *karMAny slaVAR'*
▪ a Russian-English dictionary	**русско-английский словарь** *RUska-anGLIYski slaVAR'*
Where can I find ____ ?	**Где можно найти ____ ?** *GDYE MOZHna nayTI*
▪ children's books	**детские книги** *DYETskiye KNIgi*

▪ art books	**книги по искусству**	*KNIgi pa iSKUSTvu*
▪ a collection of stories	**сборник рассказов**	*ZBORnik raSKAzaf*
▪ a collection of poetry	**сборник стихотворений**	*ZBORnik stikhatvaRYEni*
▪ a history book	**книгу по истории**	*KNIgu pa iSTOrii*
▪ a novel in translation	**роман в переводе**	*raMAN f piriVOdye*
I'll take these books.	**Я возьму эти книги.**	*YA vaz'MU Eti KNIgi*
How much do they cost?	**Сколько они стоят?**	*SKOL'ka aNI STOyit*
Could you write it down, please.	**Запишите мне это, пожалуйста.**	*zapiSHYtye MNYE Eta paZHAlusta*
Wrap them up, please.	**Заверните их, пожалуйста.**	*zavirNItye IKH paZHAlusta*

CLOTHING (ОДЕЖДА)

Would you please show me ____ .	**Покажите мне, пожалуйста ____ .**	*pakaZHYtye MNYE paZHAlusta*
▪ a belt	**пояс (ремень)**	*POyas (riMYEN')*
▪ a blouse	**блузку**	*BLUSku*
▪ a bra	**бюстгальтер**	*byustGAL'tir*
▪ a dress	**платье**	*PLAt'ye*
▪ a coat	**пальто**	*pal'TO*
▪ a fur coat	**шубу**	*SHUbu*
▪ a fur hat	**меховую шапку**	*mikhaVUyu SHAPku*
▪ gloves	**перчатки**	*pirCHATki*
▪ a handkerchief	**носовой платок**	*nasaVOY plaTOK*
▪ a hat	**шапку**	*SHAPku*

a jacket	пиджак *pidZHAK*
jeans	джинсы *DZHYNsy*
mittens	рукавицы *rukaVItsy*
panties (ladies')	трусики *TRUsiki*
pants	брюки *BRYUki*
pantyhose	колготки *kalGOTki*
a raincoat	плащ *PLASH*
a robe	халат *khaLAT*
a scarf	шарф *SHARF*
a shirt	сорочку (**рубашку**) *saROCHku* (*ruBASHku*)
(a pair of) shoes	обувь *Obuf'*
a skirt	юбку *YUPku*
shorts (men's briefs)	трусы *truSY*
a slip	комбинацию *kambiNAtsiyu*
a half-slip	нижнюю юбку *NIZHnyuyu YUPku*
slippers	тапочки *TApachki*

■ socks	носки	*naSKI*
■ stockings	чулки	*chulKI*
■ a suit	костюм	*kaSTYUM*
■ a sweater	свитер	*SVItir*
■ a tie	галстук	*GALstuk*
■ an undershirt	майку	*MAYku*
■ a wallet	бумажник	*buMAZHnik*

Do you have anything ____ ?	У вас есть что-нибудь ____ ?	*u VAS YEST' SHTO-nibut'*
■ with long sleeves	с длинными рукавами	*z DLInymi rukaVAmi*
■ with short sleeves	с короткими рукавами	*s kaROTkimi rukaVAmi*
■ cheaper	подешевле	*padiSHEvlye*
■ else	ещё	*yiSHO*
■ larger	побольше	*paBOL'she*
■ more expensive	подороже	*padaROzhe*
■ longer	подлиннее	*padliNYEye*
■ of better quality	лучшего качества	*LUCHshiva KAchistva*
■ shorter	покороче	*pakaROche*
■ smaller	поменьше	*paMYEN'she*

Where are the sale items?	Где товары по сниженным ценам?	*GDYE taVAry pa SNIzhinym tsiNAM*
I don't like the color.	Мне не нравится цвет.	*MNYE NYE NRAvitsa TSVYET*
Do you have it in ____ ?	У вас есть ____ ?	*u VAS YEST'*
■ black	чёрный	*CHORny*
■ dark blue	синий	*SIni*
■ light blue	голубой	*galuBOY*
■ brown	коричневый	*kaRICHnivy*

■ gray	**серый**	*SYEry*
■ green	**зелёный**	*ziLYOny*
■ pink	**розовый**	*ROzavy*
■ red	**красный**	*KRASny*
■ white	**белый**	*BYEly*
■ yellow	**жёлтый**	*ZHOLty*

It doesn't fit me. **Это не мой размер.** *Eta NYE MOY razMYER*

It fits me well. **Это на меня сидит хорошо.** *Eta na miNYA siDIT kharaSHO*

I take size ____ . **Мой размер ____ .** *MOY razMYER*

May I try it on? **Можно примерить?** *MOZHna priMYErit'*

Where are the changing rooms? **Где примерочные кабины?** *GDYE priMYErachniye kaBIny*

I need a ____ . **Мне нужен ____ .** *MNYE NUzhin*

■ small	**маленький размер**	*MAlin'ki razMYER*
■ medium	**средний размер**	*SRYEDni razMYER*
■ large	**большой размер**	*bal'SHOY razMYER*

I'll take it. **Я возьму.** *YA vaz'MU*

FABRICS (ТКАНИ)

chiffon	**шифон**	*shiFON*
corduroy	**рубчатый вельвет**	*RUPchaty vil'VYET*
cotton	**хлопчатобумажная ткань** *khlapchatabuMAZHnaya TKAN'*	
felt	**войлок**	*VOYlak*

flannel	**фланель** *flaNYEL'*
fur	**мех** *MYEKH*
◼ fox	**лиса** *liSA*
◼ rabbit	**кролик** *KROlik*
◼ mink	**норка** *NORka*
◼ sheepskin	**овчина** *afCHIna*
◼ marmot	**сурок** *suROK*
◼ sable	**соболь** *SObal'*
◼ wolf	**волк** *VOLK*
gabardine	**габардин** *gabarDIN*
lace	**кружева** *kruzhiVA*
leather	**кожа** *KOzha*
linen	**полотно** *palatNO*
nylon	**нейлон** *niyLON*
permanent press	**плиссированная ткань** *plisiROvanaya TKAN'*
polyester	**полиэфир** *palieFIR*
poplin	**поплин** *paPLIN*
rayon	**вискоза** *viSKOza*
sateen	**сатин** *saTIN*
satin	**атлас** *atLAS*
silk	**шёлк** *SHOLK*
suede	**замша** *ZAMsha*
terrycloth	**махровая ткань** *maKHROvaya TKAN'*
velvet	**бархат** *BARkhat*
velveteen	**вельвет** *vil'VYET*
wash-and-wear	**немнущаяся ткань** *niMNUshayasya TKAN'*
wool	**шерсть** *SHERST'*

Show me something _____ .	**Покажите мне что-нибудь _____ .** *pakaZHYtye MNYE SHTO-nibut'*
■ in a solid color	**однотонное** *adnaTOnaye*
■ with stripes	**в полоску** *f paLOSku*
■ with polka dots	**в горошек** *v gaROshik*
■ in plaid	**в клетку** *f KLYETku*
■ in herringbone	**в ёлочку** *v YOlachku*
■ checked	**в шашечку** *f SHAshichku*

SHOES AND BOOTS (ОБУВЬ)

I want to look at (men's) shoes.	**Я хочу смотреть ботинки.** *YA khaCHU smaTRYET' baTINki*
I want to look at (women's) shoes.	**Я хочу смотреть туфли.** *YA khaCHU smaTRYET' TUfli*
I want to buy a pair of boots.	**Я хочу купить пару сапог.** *YA khaCHU kuPIT' PAru saPOK*
I don't know my size.	**Я не знаю какой размер.** *YA NYE ZNAyu kaKOY razMYER*
These are too big.	**Они мне велики.** *aNI MNYE viliKI*
These are too narrow.	**Они мне тесны.** *aNI MNYE tiSNY*
These are too small.	**Они мне малы.** *aNI MNYE maLY*
These are too wide.	**Они мне широки.** *aNI MNYE shiraKI*
They pinch me.	**Они меня жмут.** *aNI miNYA ZHMUT*
They fit me.	**Они мне как раз.** *aNI MNYE KAK RAS*
I'll take them.	**Я их возьму.** *YA IKH vaz'MU*
I also need shoelaces.	**Мне также нужны шнурки.** *MNYE TAGzhe nuzhNY shnurKI*

When you shop for clothes in Russia you must be aware that there are great variations in sizes. It is helpful if you know your height (**рост** *ROST*) and chest (**обхват груди** *apKHVAT GRUdi*) and waist (**обхват талии** *apKHVAT TAlii*) measurements in centimeters in order to use the conversion charts found in many department and clothing stores. In any case you should try on the item. Ask for the changing booths—**примерочные кабины** *priMYErachniye kaBIny*.

ELECTRICAL APPLIANCES (ЭЛЕКТРОТОВАРЫ)

Soviet electrical appliances operate on 220-volt current, except for some outlets for electric shavers and hair dryers in hotel rooms. To use 110-volt electrical appliances you will need a converter, and you will also need an adapter plug to enable European or American plugs to fit Russian sockets. Alternatively, you might purchase a hair dryer or electric shaver with dual voltage.

I want to buy ____ .	**Я хочу купить ____ .**	*YA khaCHU kuPIT'*
an adapter	**адаптер**	*aDAPtir*
a battery	**батарею**	*bataRYEyu*
a blender	**сокавыжиматель**	*sakavyzhiMAtil'*
an electric shaver	**электрическую бритву**	*elikTRIchiskuyu BRITvu*
an extension cord	**шнур-удлинитель**	*SHNUR-udliNItil'*
a hair dryer	**фен**	*FYEN*
a plug	**вилку**	*VILku*
a radio	**радио**	*RAdio*
a record player	**проигрыватель**	*praIgrivatil'*
a cassette recorder	**магнитофон**	*magnitaFON*

▦ a (color) television	**(цветной) телевизор** *(tsvitNOY)* *tiliVIzar*
▦ a VCR	**видео-магнитофон** *VIdio-magnitaFON*
▦ a toaster	**тостер** *TOStir*
▦ a transformer	**трансформатор** *transfarMAtar*
It doesn't work.	**Он не работает.** *ON NYE raBOtayit*
Can you repair this?	**Вы можете это починить?** *VY MOzhitye Eta pachiNIT'*

FOOD (ГАСТРОНОМ) HOUSEHOLD ITEMS (ХОЗЯЙСТВЕННЫЕ ТОВАРЫ)

When you set out for the stores, bring along a plastic bag or, even better, a net bag. Russians have a name for this bag—**авоська** *aVOS'ka* (just in case). Some items will be wrapped in plain gray or brown paper, but you'll find it more convenient to carry them in the bag. Many food stores are self-service, but in others you'll need to determine the price of what you want, then tell the cashier and pay. Only after you have a receipt can you line up to obtain the item.

Please give me ____ .	**Дайте мне, пожалуйста, ____ .** *DAYtye MNYE paZHAlusta*
▦ a bar of soap	**кусок мыла** *kuSOK MYla*
▦ a bottle of juice	**бутылку сока** *buTYLku SOka*
▦ a box of cereal	**пакет крупы** *paKYET kruPY*
▦ a can of tomato sauce	**банку томатного соуса** *BANku taMATnava SOUsa*
▦ ten eggs	**десяток яиц** *diSYAtak yaITS*
▦ a jar of coffee	**банку кофе** *BANku KOfye*

- a kilo of potatoes **кило картошки** *kiLO karTOSHki*
- a half-kilo of cherries **пол-кило вишни** *POL-kiLO VISHni*
- a liter of milk **литр молока** *LITR malaKA*
- a box of candy **коробку конфет** *kaROPku kanFYET*
- 100 grams of cheese **сто грамм сыра** *STO GRAM SYra*
- 200 grams of salami **двести грамм колбасы** *DVYESti GRAM kalbaSY*
- a roll of toilet paper **рулон туалетной бумаги** *ruLON tuaLYETnay buMAgi*

METRIC WEIGHTS AND MEASURES

	SOLID MEASURES		
	(approximate measurements only)		
	Grams	Grams	
Ounces	**(Грамм)**	**(Грамм)**	Ounces
¼	7	10	⅓
½	14	100	3½
¾	21	300	10½
1	28	450	16 (1 lb.)
	Kilograms	Kilograms	
Pounds	**(Килограмм)**	**(Килограмм)**	Pounds
1	½	1	2¼
5	2¼	3	6½
10	4½	5	11
20	9	10	22
50	23	50	110
100	45	100	220

	LIQUID MEASURES (approximate measurements only)		
Ounces	Milliliters (Грамм)	Milliliters (Грамм)	Ounces
1	30	10	⅓
6	175	50	1½
12	350	100	3½
16	475	150	5
32	900	250	8½
Gallons	Liters (Литр)	Liters (Литр)	Gallons
1	3¾	1	¼ (1 quart)
5	19	5	1⅓
10	38	10	2½

Note: Common measurements for purchasing food are one kilo (one kilogram = one thousand grams) or some multiple of one hundred grams: **сто грамм, двести грамм.** Russians also use grams instead of milliliters for liquid measurement. A common measure of vodka is 100 grams.

JEWELRY (ЮВЕЛИРНЫЙ МАГАЗИН)

We would like to see ____ .	Мы хотели бы посмотреть ____ . *MY khaTYEli BY pasmaTRYET'*
some beads	**бусы** *BUsy*
a bracelet	**браслет** *braSLYET*
a brooch	**брошь** *BROSH*
a chain	**цепочку** *tsiPOCHku*
a charm	**брелок** *briLOK*
some earrings	**серьги** *SYER'gi*
a necklace	**ожерелье** *azhiRYEl'ye*

▦ a pin	**булавку** *buLAFku*	
▦ a ring	**кольцо** *kal'TSO*	
▦ a wedding/ engagement ring	**обручальное кольцо** *abruCHAL'naye kal'TSO*	
▦ a watch	**часы** *chiSY*	
▦ a digital watch	**электронные часы** *elikTROniye chiSY*	
Is this ____ ?	**Это ____ ?** *Eta*	
▦ gold	**золото** *ZOlata*	
▦ platinum	**платина** *PLAtina*	
▦ silver	**серебро** *siriBRO*	
▦ stainless steel	**нержавейка** *nirzhaVEYka*	
Is it solid gold or gold plated?	**Это золото или позолоченое?** *Eta ZOlata Ili pazaLOchinaye*	
How many carats?	**Сколько каратов?** *SKOL'ka kaRAtaf*	
What is this stone?	**Что это за камень?** *SHTO Eta za KAmin'*	
I like ____ .	**Я люблю ____ .** *YA lyuBLYU*	
▦ amber	**янтарь** *yanTAR'*	
▦ amethyst	**аметист** *amiTIST*	
▦ aquamarine	**аквамарин** *akvamaRIN*	
▦ diamond	**бриллиант** *briliANT*	
▦ emerald	**изумруд** *izumRUT*	
▦ ivory	**слоновую кость** *SLOnavuyu KOST'*	
▦ jade	**нефрит** *niFRIT*	
▦ jasper	**яшму** *YASHmu*	
▦ malachite	**малахит** *malaKHIT*	
▦ onyx	**оникс** *Oniks*	
▦ pearls	**жемчуг** *zhimCHUK*	
▦ ruby	**рубин** *ruBIN*	

■ sapphire	**сапфир** *sapFIR*
■ topaz	**топаз** *taPAS*
■ tourmaline	**турмалин** *turmaLIN*
■ turquoise	**бирюзу** *biRYUzu*
I like this ring.	**Мне нравится это кольцо.** *MNYE NRAvitsa Eta kal'TSO*
How much does it cost?	**Сколько оно стоит?** *SKOL'ka aNO STOit*

MUSICAL RECORDS (ПЛАСТИНКИ)

Is there a record shop nearby?	**Есть поблизости магазин "Граммпластинки"?** *YEST' paBLIzasti magaZIN gramplaSTINki*
Do you sell ____ ?	**Вы продаёте ____ ?** *VY pradaYOtye*
■ cartridges	**головки** *gaLOFki*
■ cassettes	**кассеты** *kaSYEty*
■ needles	**иголки** *iGOLki*
■ records	**пластинки** *plaSTINki*
■ compact discs	**компактные диски** *kamPAKTniye DISki*
Is this record ____ ?	**Эта пластинка ____ ?** *Eta plaSTINka*
■ 33 RPM	**на тридцать три оборота** *na TRItsat' TRI abaROta*
■ 45 RPM	**на сорок пять оборотов** *na SOrak PYAT' abaROtaf*
Where is the ____ section?	**Где отдел ____ ?** *GDYE aDYEL*
■ "Russian Music"	**Русская музыка** *RUskaya MUzyka*
■ "Classical Music"	**Классическая музыка** *klaSIchiskaya MUzyka*

■	"Folk Music"	**Народная музыка** *naRODnaya MUzyka*
■	"Latest Hits"	**Популярная (современная) музыка** *papuLYARnaya (savriMYEnaya) MUzyka*
■	"Opera and Ballet"	**Опера и балет** *Opira I baLYET*

NEWSSTAND

Do you have any newspapers in English?	**У вас есть газеты на английском?** *U VAS YEST' gaZYEty na anGLIYskam*
Show me some magazines in English!	**Покажите мне журналы на английском!** *pakaZHYtye MNYE zhurNAly na anGLIYskam*
These postcards, please!	**Эти открытки, пожалуйста!** *Eti atKRYTki paZHAlusta*
Do you have stamps?	**У вас есть марки?** *u VAS YEST' MARki*
How much do I owe?	**Сколько с меня?** *SKOL'ka s miNYA*

> The little lapel pins that Russians wear make great souvenirs at very modest prices. These pins—**значки** *znachKI*—can be purchased at most kiosks. Often they come as a set—**набор**   *naBOR*. You might take some pins from your organization, state, or town as gifts for your hosts and Russian acquaintances.

PHOTOGRAPHIC SUPPLIES (ФОТОТОВАРЫ)

Where is a camera shop?	**Где здесь фототовары?** *GDYE ZDYES' fotataVAry*
Do you develop film?	**Вы проявляете плёнку?** *VY prayaVLYAyitye PLYONku*

I have two rolls.	**У меня две плёнки.** *U miNYA DVYE PLYONki*
Please print them all!	**Напечатайте все!** *napiCHAtaytye FSYE*
Can you enlarge this one?	**Вы можете эту увеличить?** *VY MOzhitye Etu uviLIchit'*
glossy finish	**гланц** *GLANTS*
matte finish	**матовый** *MAtavy*
color film, 20 exposures	**цветную плёнку, двадцать кадров** *tsvitNUyu PLYONku, DVAtsat' KAdraf*
black and white film, 36 exposures	**черно-белую плёнку, тридцать шесть кадров** *CHORna-BYEluyu PLYONku, TRItsat' SHEST' KAdraf*
for slides	**на слайды** *na SLAYdy*
ASA 100	**ГОСТ 100** *GOST STO*

Russian film can be purchased with or without a cartridge. Many stores will have a black box where you can unpack and wind your own film, but if you are not familiar with the process, ask for film already wound on the cassette —**в кассете** *f kaSYEtye*.

Do you repair cameras?	**Вы чините фотоаппараты?** *VY chiNItye fotaapaRAty*
I need a battery for my flash.	**Мне нужна батарея для вспышки.** *MNYE nuzhNA bataRYEya dlya FSPYSHki*

SOUVENIRS

For fine Russian souvenirs, check the specialty shops, and don't forget the one at the airport before you depart. Some of the traditional Russian handicrafts are painted wooden dishes from the city of Khokhloma and exquisite lacquered boxes from Palekh and Mstyora. You may also want to buy some of the fine linen items or filigree work, and you certainly don't want to forget caviar and vodka for friends back home. You will also be able to find Western cigarettes, perfumes, and alcoholic beverages in the Beriozka shop.

I want to purchase a _____ .	**Я хочу купить _____ .**	*YA khaCHU kuPIT'*
special gift	**особый подарок**	*aSOby paDArak*
small souvenir	**маленький сувенир**	*MAlin'ki suviNIR*
It's for _____ .	**Он для _____ .**	*ON dlya*
my daughter	**моей дочки**	*maYEY DOCHki*
my father	**моего отца**	*mayiVO aTSA*
my husband	**моего мужа**	*mayiVO MUzha*
my mother	**моей матери**	*maYEY MAtiri*
my son	**моего сына**	*mayiVO SYna*
my wife	**моей жены**	*maYEY zhiNY*
Would you show me some _____ !	**Покажите мне _____ !**	*pakaZHYtye MNYE*
blown glass	**художественное стекло**	*khuDOzhistvinaye stiKLO*
carved objects	**резьбу**	*riz'BU*
crystal	**хрусталь**	*khruSTAL'*
nested dolls	**матрёшки**	*maTRYOSHki*
ceramics	**керамику**	*kiRAmiku*
fans	**веера**	*viyiRA*
jewelry	**ювелирные изделия**	*yuviLIRniye izDYEliya*
lace	**кружева**	*kruzhiVA*
leather goods	**изделия из кожи**	*izDYEliya is KOzhi*
liqueurs	**ликёры**	*liKYOry*
musical instruments	**музыкальные инструменты**	*muzyKAL'niye instruMYENty*

■	perfumes	**духи** *duKHI*
■	pictures	**картины** *karTIny*
■	posters	**плакаты** *plaKAty*

How do you want to pay?	**Чем вы будете платить?** *CHEM VY BUditye plaTIT'*
With cash?	**Наличными?** *naLICHnymi*
With a credit card?	**Кредитной карточкой?** *kriDITnay KARtachkay*

STATIONERY (КАНЦЕЛЯРСКИЕ ТОВАРЫ)

	I want to buy ____ .	**Я хочу купить ____ .** *YA khaCHU kuPIT'*
■	a ball-point pen	**ручку** *RUCHku*
■	a deck of cards	**колоду карт** *kaLOdu KART*
■	drawing paper	**бумагу для рисования** *buMAgu dlya risaVAniya*
■	an envelope	**конверт** *kanVYERT*
■	an eraser	**ластик** *LAStik*
■	glue	**клей** *KLYEY*
■	a notebook	**тетрадь** *tiTRAT'*
■	a pencil	**карандаш** *karanDASH*
■	a pencil sharpener	**точилку** *taCHILku*
■	a ruler	**линейку** *liNYEYku*
■	Scotch tape	**скотч (клеющую ленту)** *SKOTCH (KLYEyushuyu LYENtu)*
■	string	**шпагат** *shpaGAT*
■	typing paper	**бумагу для пишущей машинки** *buMAgu dlya PIshushey maSHYNki*
■	a writing pad	**блокнот** *blakNOT*

■ writing paper	**бумагу для писем** *buMAgu dlya PIsim*
■ thumbtacks	**кнопки** *KNOPki*
■ paperclips	**скрепки** *SKRYEPki*
■ rubber bands	**резинки** *riZINki*

TOBACCO (ТАБАК)

A pack of cigarettes, please.	**Пачку сигарет, пожалуйста.** *PACHku sigaRYET paZHAlusta*
■ filtered	**с фильтром** *s FIL'tram*
■ unfiltered	**без фильтра** *byes FIL'tra*
■ menthol	**с ментолом** *s minTOlam*
■ king-size (long)	**кинг-сайз (длинные)** *KING-SAYS (DLIniye)*
Are these cigarettes strong?	**Эти сигареты крепкие?** *Eti sigaRYEty KRYEPkiye*
Are they mild?	**Они слабые?** *aNI SLAbiye*
Do you have American cigarettes?	**У вас есть американские сигареты?** *u VAS YEST' amiriKANskiye sigaRYEty*
What brands?	**Какие марки?** *kaKIye MARki*
And a pack of matches, please.	**И спички, пожалуйста.** *I SPICHki paZHAlusta*
Do you carry _____ ?	**У вас есмь _____ ?** *u VAS YEST'*
■ butane gas	**газ** *GAS*
■ chewing tobacco	**махорка** *maKHORka*
■ cigarette holders	**мундштуки** *muntSHTUki*
■ cigars	**сигары** *siGAry*
■ flints	**кремни** *krimNI*

lighters	**зажигалки** *zazhiGALki*
pipes	**трубки** *TRUPki*
pipe tobacco	**трубочный табак** *TRUbachny taBAK*

TOILETRIES (ПАРФЮМЕРИЯ)

Do you have ___ ?	**У вас есть ___ ?** *u VAS YEST'*
after shave	**лосьон после бритья** *laS'YON POslye briT'YA*
bobby pins	**шпильки заколки** *SHPILki zaKOLki*
a brush	**щётка** *SHOTka*
cleansing cream	**крем для очистки кожи** *KRYEM dlya aCHISTki KOzhi*
nourishing cream	**питательный крем** *piTAtil'ny KRYEM*
cologne	**одеколон** *adikaLON*
a comb	**расчёска** *rasCHOSka*
a deodorant	**дезодорант** *dizadaRANT*
disposable diapers	**бумажные пелёнки** *buMAZHniye piLYONki*
eye liner	**карандаш для бровей** *karanDASH dlya braVYEY*
eyebrow pencil	**карандаш для век** *karanDASH dlya VYEK*
eye shadow	**тени** *TYEni*
face lotion	**лосьон** *laS'YON*
hair spray	**лак для волос** *LAK dlya vaLOS*
lip gloss	**блеск для губ** *BLYESK dlya GUP*
lipstick	**губная помада** *gubNAya paMAda*
make-up	**крем-пудра (мэйк-ап)** *KRYEM-PUdra (meyk-AP)*

▓ mascara	**тушь для ресниц**	*TUSH dlya riSNITS*
▓ a mirror	**зеркало**	*ZYERkala*
▓ mouth wash	**зубной эликсир**	*zubNOY elikSIR*
▓ nail clippers	**кусачки**	*kuSACHki*
▓ a nail file	**пилка**	*PILka*
▓ nail polish	**лак для ногтей**	*LAK dlya nakTYEY*
▓ nail polish remover	**ацетон**	*atsiTON*
▓ a razor	**бритва**	*BRITva*
▓ razor blades	**лезвия**	*LYEZviya*
▓ rouge	**румяна**	*ruMYAna*
▓ sanitary napkins	**гигиенические салфетки**	*gigiyiNIchiskiye salFYETki*
▓ (cuticle) scissors	**маникюрные ножницы**	*maniKYURniye NOZHnitsy*
▓ shampoo	**шампунь**	*shamPUN'*
▓ a sponge	**губка**	*GUPka*
▓ talcum powder	**тальк**	*TAL'K*
▓ tampons	**тампоны (марлевые салфетки)**	*tamPOny (MARliviye salFYETki)*
▓ tissues	**салфетки**	*salFYETki*
▓ toilet paper	**туалетная бумага**	*tuaLYETnaya buMAga*
▓ a toothbrush	**зубная щётка**	*zubNAya SHOTka*
▓ toothpaste	**зубная паста**	*zubNAya PASta*
▓ tweezers	**щипчики**	*SHIPchiki*

PERSONAL CARE AND SERVICES

If your hotel doesn't offer these services, ask the desk clerk to recommend a place nearby.

BARBER SHOP (ПАРИКМАХЕРСКАЯ)

Where is a good barber shop?	**Где хорошая парикмахерская?** *GDYE khaROshaya parikMAkhirskaya*
Does the hotel have a barber shop?	**В гостинице есть парикмахерская?** *v gaSTInitse YEST' parikMAkhirskaya*
Do I have to wait long?	**Надо долго ждать?** *NAda DOLga ZHDAT'*
Whose turn is it?	**Чья очередь?** *CH'YA Ochirit'*
I want a shave.	**Я хочу побриться.** *YA khaCHU paBRItsa*
I want a haircut.	**Я хочу постричься.** *YA khaCHU paSTRICHsa*
A shampoo, please.	**Помойте, пожалуйста, голову.** *paMOYtye paZHAlusta GOlavu*
Short in back, long in front.	**Сзади коротко, спереди длинно.** *ZAdi KOratka SPYEridi DLIna*
Leave it long.	**Оставьте эту длину.** *aSTAF'tye Etu dliNU*
I want it (very) short.	**(Очень) коротко.** *(Ochin') KOratka*
You can cut a little ____ .	**Можно покороче ____ .** *MOZHna pakaROche*
▪ in back	**сзади** *ZAdi*
▪ in front	**спереди** *SPYEridi*
▪ off the top	**сверху** *SFYERkhu*
▪ on the sides	**по бокам** *pa baKAM*

I have a part ____ .	**У меня пробор ____ .** *u miNYA praBOR*
on the left	**слева** *SLYEva*
on the right	**справа** *SPRAva*
in the middle	**прямой** *priMOY*
I comb my hair ____ .	**Я зачёсываю волосы ____ .** *YA zaCHOsyvayu VOlasy*
straight back	**прямо назад** *PRYAma naZAT*
without a part	**без пробора** *byes praBOra*
Cut a little bit more here.	**Здесь чуть-чуть покороче.** *ZDYES' CHUT'-CHUT' pakaROche*
That's fine.	**Так хорошо.** *TAK kharaSHO*
I don't want ____ .	**Не надо ____ .** *NYE NAda*
a wash	**мытья** *myT'YA*
eau de Cologne	**одеколона** *adikaLOna*
Use the scissors only.	**Только ножницами.** *TOL'ka NOZHnitsami*
A razor cut.	**Бритвой, пожалуйста.** *BRITvay paZHAlusta*
You can use the electric razor.	**Можно электрической бритвой.** *MOZHna elikTRIchiskay BRITvay*
Please trim ____ .	**Подстригите ____ .** *padstriGItye*
Please even out ____ .	**Подравняйте ____ .** *padravNYAYtye*
my beard	**бороду** *BOradu*
my moustache	**усы** *uSY*
my sideburns	**височки** *viSOCHki*
Please shave the back of my neck.	**Побрейте шею.** *paBRYEYtye SHEyu*
Where is a mirror?	**Где здесь зеркало?** *GDYE ZDYES' ZYERkala*
I want to look at myself.	**Хочу на себя взглянуть.** *khaCHU na siBYA vzgliNUT'*

How much do I owe you?	**Сколько я вам должен?** *SKOL'ka YA VAM DOLzhin*

BEAUTY PARLOR
(ЖЕНСКАЯ ПАРИКМАХЕРСКАЯ)

Is there a beauty parlor near here?	**Поблизости есть женская парикмахерская?** *paBLIzasti YEST' ZHENskaya parikMAkhirskaya*
Can I make an appointment ____ ?	**Можно записаться ____ ?** *MOZHna zapiSAtsa*
▪ for today	**на сегодня** *na siVODnya*
▪ after lunch	**после обеда** *POslye aBYEda*
▪ tomorrow	**на завтра** *na ZAFtra*
What would you like to have done?	**Что вам сделать?** *SHTO VAM ZDYElat'*
A color rinse?	**Окраску волос?** *aKRASku vaLOS*
A facial massage?	**Массаж лица?** *maSASH liTSA*

A haircut?	**Стрижку?** *STRISHku*
A manicure?	**Маникюр?** *maniKYUR*
A permanent?	**Химическую завивку?** *khiMIchiskuyu zaVIFku*
A shampoo?	**Мытьё?** *myT'YO*
A tint?	**Тон?** *TON*
A touch up?	**Поправку?** *paPRAFku*
A wash and set?	**Мытьё и укладку?** *myT'YO I uKLATku*
No, don't cut it.	**Нет, стричь не надо.** *NYET STRICH NYE NAda*
What color?	**Какого цвета?** *kaKOva TSVYEta*
█ auburn	**каштановый** *kashTAnavy*
█ blond	**белокурый** *bilaKUry*
█ brunette	**брюнетка** *bryuNYETka*
█ a darker color	**потемнее** *patimNYEye*
█ a lighter color	**посветлее** *pasvitLYEye*
Don't use any hairspray.	**Без лака, пожалуйста.** *byez LAka paZHAlusta*
Just a little.	**Совсем мало.** *safSYEM MAla*
A little more.	**Побольше.** *paBOL'she*
Give me a new (stylish) hairdo.	**Сделайте мне модную причёску.** *ZDYElaytye MNYE MODnuyu priCHOSku*
Something striking _____ .	**Что-нибудь экстравагантное _____ .** *SHTO-nibut' ekstravaGANTnaye*
█ with curls	**с кудрями** *s KUdryami*
█ with waves	**с волнами** *s valNAmi*
█ with bangs	**с чёлкой** *s CHOLkay*
In a bun on top.	**Пучок.** *puCHOK*
A pony tail?	**Хвост?** *KHVOST*

BATHHOUSE (БАНЯ)

One of the true pleasures in Russia is a visit to the bathhouse, or **баня** *BAnya*. Take shampoo, soap, a change of underwear, and a towel with you. Be prepared to spend a few hours spoiling yourself. At the entrance to the bathhouse you'll see vendors selling bunches of oak or birch twigs (**веник** *VYEnik*). These are a must, so buy a bunch. Inside you purchase a ticket, then proceed to the changing rooms, where you can leave your clothes in a locker. Find a wash-basin (**тазик** *TAzik*), and you are ready to begin. Wet yourself down, then go into the steam room (**парильня** *paRIL'nya*). It is hottest at the top, so move up gradually. After a few minutes of sweating, go outside and take a cool dip in the pool, then return to the steam room. Russians suggest that this ritual be performed three times. Finally, you'll bathe and shampoo your hair. Then the old-timers recommend that you sit a while (maybe have a cool drink) so your body can adjust to normal room temperature. Oh, yes! Smack the twigs against your skin to improve the circulation. For hard-to-reach places, it is acceptable to ask your neighbor for assistance. The baths can also provide a number of services, such as pressing clothes and doing minor repairs. Some may offer a barber shop and beauty parlor with manicures and pedicures.

I'll take some twigs.	**Веник, пожалуйста.** *VYEnik paZHAlusta*	
One ticket please.	**Один билет, пожалуйста.** *aDIN biLYET paZHAlusta*	
Can I leave my valuables?	**Можно сдавать ценные вещи?** *MOZHna zdaVAT' TSEniye VYEshi*	
Please bring me ____ .	**Принесите мне, пожалуйста ____ .** *priniSItye MNYE paZHAlusta*	
■ some slippers	**тапочки** *TApachki*	
■ a bar of soap	**кусок мыла** *kuSOK MYla*	
■ a linen towel	**простыню** *praSTYnyu*	
■ a sponge	**мочалку** *maCHALku*	

■ some shampoo	**шампунь** *shamPUN'*
■ a wrap-around	**накидку** *naKITku*
May I take this washbasin?	**Можно взять этот тазик?** *MOZHna VZYAT' Etat TAzik*
Where is the steam room?	**Где парильня?** *GDYE paRIL'nya*
It's too hot for me up there.	**Там мне слишком жарко.** *TAM MNYE SLISHkam ZHARka*
Where is the swimming pool?	**Где бассейн?** *GDYE baSYEYN*
Where are the showers?	**Где душ?** *GDYE DUSH*
Is there a sauna here?	**Здесь есть сауна?** *ZDYES' YEST' SAUna*
Do you have a buffet?	**У вас есть буфет?** *u VAS YEST' buFYET*

LAUNDRY AND DRY CLEANING
(ПРАЧЕЧНАЯ И ХИМЧИСТКА)

You may be able to have shirts, blouses, and underwear washed at the hotel. Usually one of the maids will do it for a modest price. There also will probably be an ironing board and iron on your floor. Simply ask the "key lady" (**дежурная** *diZHURnaya*). Otherwise you can use the laundromat and dry cleaner's.

Where is the nearest laundry?	**Где ближайшая прачечная?** *GDYE bliZHAYshaya PRAchichnaya*
Where is a laundromat?	**Где прачечная самообслуживания?** *GDYE PRAchichnaya samaapSLUzhivaniya*
I have a lot of clothes to be ____ .	**У меня набралась большая ____ .** *U miNYA nabraLAS' bal'SHAya*
■ dry cleaned	**чистка** *CHISTka*
■ washed	**стирка** *STIRka*
■ ironed	**глажка** *GLASHka*

Here's the list:	**Вот список:**	*VOT SPIsak*
▢ three shirts	**три рубашки**	*TRI ruBASHki*
▢ ten handkerchiefs	**десять носовых платков**	*DYEsit' nasaVYKH platKOF*
▢ six pairs of socks	**шесть пар носков**	*SHEST' PAR naSKOF*
▢ one blouse	**одна блузка**	*aDNA BLUSka*
▢ panties	**трусики**	*TRUsiki*
▢ three pajamas	**три пижамы**	*TRI piZHAmy*
▢ one suit	**один костюм**	*aDIN kaSTYUM*
▢ five ties	**пять галстуков**	*PYAT' GALstukaf*
▢ two dresses	**два платья**	*DVA PLAt'ya*
▢ one sweater	**один свитер**	*aDIN SVItir*
▢ a pair of gloves	**перчатки**	*pirCHATki*
I need them ____ .	**Мне нужно ____ .**	*MNYE NUZHna*
▢ tonight	**к вечеру**	*k VYEchiru*
▢ tomorrow	**завтра**	*ZAFtra*
▢ the day after tomorrow	**послезавтра**	*pasliZAFtra*
When will you bring them back?	**Когда вы их принесёте?**	*kagDA VY IKH priniSYOtye*
When will it be ready?	**Когда будет готово?**	*kagDA BUdit gaTOva*
There is a spot on the blouse.	**На блузке есть пятно.**	*na BLUSkye YEST' pitNO*
There's a button missing.	**Здесь нет пуговицы.**	*ZDYES' NYET PUgavitsy*
Can you sew it back on?	**Не могли бы вы пришить?**	*NYE maGLI BY VY priSHYT'*
These aren't my things.	**Это не мои вещи.**	*Eta NYE maYI VYEshi*

SHOE REPAIRS (РЕМОНТ ОБУВИ)

All around town you are likely to see tiny shoe shine and repair booths. Why not step inside and treat yourself to a shine? At the booths you can have minor repairs performed. For major repairs, bring your shoes or boots to the shoe repair shops.

A shoe shine please.	**Почистите, пожалуйста.** *PaCHIStitye paZHAlusta*
Can you fix these _____ ?	**Вы можете починить _____ ?** *VY MOzhitye pachiNIT'*
ladies' shoes	**туфли** *TUfli*
shoes	**ботинки** *baTINki*
boots	**сапоги** *sapaGI*
Just soles.	**Только подмётки.** *TOL'ka padMYOTki*
Heels, please.	**Каблуки, пожалуйста.** *kabluKI paZHAlusta*
Can you do it now?	**Вы можете сейчас?** *VY MOzhitye siyCHAS*
A pair of shoe laces.	**Шнурки.** *shnurKI*
A pair of insoles.	**Стельки.** *STYEL'ki*

WATCH REPAIRS (РЕМОНТ ЧАСОВ)

Can you repair this _____ ?	**Вы можете починить _____ ?** *VY MOzhitye pachiNIT'*
clock/watch	**часы** *chiSY*
alarm clock	**будильник** *buDIL'nik*
digital watch	**электронные часы** *elikTROniye chiSY*
quartz watch	**кварцовые часы** *KVARtsaviye chiSY*
wristwatch	**наручные часы** *naRUCHniye chiSY*

There's something wrong with the ____ .	**Проблема с ____ .** *praBLYEma s*
■ glass	**стеклом** *stiKLOM*
■ hour hand	**часовой стрелкой** *chisaVOY STRYELkay*
■ minute hand	**минутной стрелкой** *miNUTnay STRYELkay*
■ second hand	**секундной стрелкой** *siKUNDnay STRYELkay*
■ stem (screw)	**головкой** *gaLOFkay*
Could you look at it?	**Вы могли бы посмотреть?** *VY maGLI BY pasmaTRYET'*
Can you replace the battery?	**Можно поставить новую батарейку?** *MOZHna paSTAvit' NOvuyu bataRYEYku*
Can you clean it?	**Можно их почистить?** *MOZHna IKH paCHIStit'*
I dropped it.	**Я их уронил.** *YA IKH uraNIL*
It doesn't run well.	**Они плохо идут.** *aNI PLOkha iDUT*
It's fast.	**Они спешат.** *aNI spiSHAT*
It's slow.	**Они отстают.** *aNI atstaYUT*
It's stopped running.	**Они стоят.** *aNI staYAT*
I wind it every day.	**Я завожу их каждый день.** *YA zavaZHU IKH KAZHdy DYEN'*

CAMERA REPAIRS (РЕМОНТ ФОТОАППАРАТОВ)

Can you fix this camera?	**Вы можете починить этот фотоаппарат?** *VY MOzhitye pachiNIT' Etat fotaapaRAT*
It doesn't work well.	**Он плохо работает.** *ON PLOkha raBOtayit*

How much will it cost?	**Сколько стоит ремонт?** *SKOL'ka STOit riMONT*
When can I come and get it?	**Когда за ним прийти?** *kagDA za NIM priyTI*
I need it as soon as possible.	**Мне нужно как можно скорее.** *MNYE NUZHna KAK MOZHna-skaRYEye*

TRAVEL TIP

A good rule of thumb about purchases is "If you see it, buy it!" You can never be certain in Russia that an item will be there the next day or that a store will be open. A variety of things—a lunch break (**перерыв на обед** *piriRYF na aBYET*), closure for inventory (**закрыт на учёт** *zaKRYT na uCHOT*), or the periodical cleaning day (**санитарный день** *saniTARny DYEN'*)—may interfere with your intentions.

MEDICAL CARE

If you are given a prescription you will need to go to a pharmacy—**аптека** *apTYEka*. Here you can also find nonprescription remedies for what ails you. Most medicines are very inexpensive. In major cities several pharmacies provide round-the-clock emergency services.

PHARMACY

Where is the nearest pharmacy?	**Где ближайшая аптека?** *GDYE bliZHAYshaya apTYEka*
When does the pharmacy ___ ?	**Когда аптека ___ ?** *kagDA apTYEka*
▓ open	**открывается** *atkryVAyitsa*
▓ close	**закрывается** *zakryVAyitsa*
Where is the prescription section?	**Где рецептный отдел?** *GDYE riTSEPTny aDYEL*
Where are the nonprescription medicines?	**Где безрецептные лекарства?** *GDYE byezriTSEPTniye liKARSTva*
I need something for ___ .	**Мне нужно что-нибудь от ___ .** *MNYE NUZHna SHTO-nibut' at*
▓ a cold	**насморка** *NASmarka*
▓ constipation	**запора** *zaPOra*
▓ a cough	**кашля** *KASHlya*
▓ diarrhea	**поноса** *paNOsa*
▓ a fever	**жара** *ZHAra*
▓ hay fever	**сенной лихорадки** *SYEnay likhaRATki*
▓ a headache	**головной боли** *galavNOY BOli*
▓ insomnia	**бессоницы** *biSOnitsy*
▓ nausea	**тошноты** *tashnaTY*
▓ sunburn	**солнечного ожога** *SOLnichnava aZHOga*

a toothache	**зубной боли** *zubNOY BOli*
an upset stomach	**желудочного расстройства** *zhiLUdachnava raSTROYSTva*
Is a prescription necessary?	**Нужен рецепт?** *NUzhin riTSEPT*
Can you fill this prescription for me?	**У вас есть лекарство по этому рецепту?** *u VAS YEST' liKARSTva pa Etamu riTSEPtu*
It's an emergency.	**Это срочно.** *Eta SROCHna*
Should I wait for it?	**Мне подождать?** *MNYE padaZHDAT'*
How long will it take?	**Сколько ждать?** *SKOL'ka ZHDAT'*
When can I come for it?	**Когда мне прийти?** *kagDA MNYE priyTI*
When should I come back?	**Когда мне вернуться?** *kagDA MNYE virNUtsa*
Do you have _____ ?	**У вас есть _____ ?** *u VAS YEST'*
adhesive tape	**пластырь** *plaSTYR'*
alcohol	**спирт** *SPIRT*
an antacid	**щёлочь** *SHOlach*
an antiseptic	**антисептик** *antiSYEPtik*
aspirin	**аспирин** *aspiRIN*
bandages	**бинт** *BINT*
cotton	**вата** *VAta*
cough drops	**таблетки от кашля** *taBLYETki at KASHlya*
cough syrup	**микстура от кашля** *mikSTUra at KASHlya*
ear drops	**ушные капли** *ushNIye KApli*
eye drops	**глазные капли** *glazNIye KApli*
iodine	**йод** *YOT*
a mild laxative	**(лёгкое) слабительное** *(LYOkaye) slaBItil'naye*

magnesia	**магнезия**	*magNYEziya*
mustard plaster	**горчичник**	*garCHICHnik*
an ointment	**мазь**	*MAS'*
a sedative	**успокаивающее**	*uspaKAivayushiye*
sleeping pills	**снотворное**	*snaTVORnaye*
suppositories	**свечи**	*SVEchi*
a thermometer	**термометр**	*tirMOmitr*
vitamins	**витамины**	*vitaMIny*

DOCTOR

In an emergency call the number for immediate care—**Скорая помощь** *SKOraya POmash*. The number in Moscow and St. Petersburg is **03**. Identify yourself as a foreigner and describe the problem, and within minutes a physician will be at your hotel. In non-emergency situations call your embassy or ask your hosts or the hotel personnel for the location of the nearest polyclinic.

I don't feel well.	**Я чувствую себя плохо.** *YA CHUSTvuyu siBYA PLOkha*
I feel sick. (*m*)	**Я заболел.** *YA zabaLYEL*
I feel sick. (*f*)	**Я заболела.** *YA zabaLYEla*
Please call a doctor.	**Вызовите, пожалуйста, врача.** *VYzavitye paZHAlusta vraCHA*
Is there a doctor who speaks English?	**Есть врач, который говорит по-английски?** *YEST' VRACH kaTOry gavaRIT pa-anGLIYski*
I'm dizzy. (My head is spinning.)	**Голова кружится.** *galaVA KRUzhitsa*
I feel weak.	**Я чувствую слабость.** *YA CHUSTvuyu SLAbast'*
I want to sit down for a while.	**Мне нужно посидеть.** *MNYE NUZHna pasiDYET'*

| My temperature is normal. | **У меня нормальная температура.**
 u miNYA narMAL'naya timpiraTUra |
| I have a high temperature. | **У меня высокая температура.**
 u miNYA vySOkaya timpiraTUra |

PARTS OF THE BODY

It hurts here.	**Болит здесь.** *baLIT ZDYES'*
My ___ hurts.	**У меня болит ___ .** *u miNYA baLIT*
abdomen	**живот** *zhiVOT*
arm	**рука** *ruKA*
back	**спина** *spiNA*
breast	**грудь** *GRUT'*
cheek	**щека** *shiKA*
ear	**ухо** *Ukha*
elbow	**локоть** *LOkat'*
eye	**глаз** *GLAS*
face	**лицо** *liTSO*
finger	**палец** *PAlits*
foot	**ступня** *stupNYA*
hand	**кисть** *KIST'*
head	**голова** *galaVA*
heart	**сердце** *SYERtse*
hip	**бедро** *biDRO*
knee	**колено** *kaLYEna*
leg	**нога** *naGA*
lip	**губа** *GUba*
mouth	**рот** *ROT*
neck	**шея** *SHEya*

■ nose	**нос**	*NOS*
■ rib	**ребро**	*riBRO*
■ shoulder	**плечо**	*pliCHO*
■ skin	**кожа**	*KOzha*
■ stomach	**желудок**	*zhiLUdak*
■ throat	**горло**	*GORla*
■ tooth	**зуб**	*ZUP*
■ wrist	**запястье**	*zaPYASt' ye*

WHAT'S WRONG

I have ___ .	**У меня ___ .**	*u miNYA*
■ an abscess	**нарыв**	*naRYV*
■ a broken bone	**перелом**	*piriLOM*
■ a bruise	**ушиб**	*uSHYP*
■ a burn	**ожог**	*aZHOK*
■ something in my eye	**что-нибудь в глазу**	*SHTO-nibut' v glaZU*
■ the chills	**озноб**	*aZNOP*
■ a chest cold	**бронхит**	*branKHIT*
■ a head cold	**насморк**	*NASmark*
■ a cough	**кашель**	*KAshil'*
■ cramps	**судороги**	*SUdaragi*
■ a cut	**порез**	*paRYES*
■ diarrhea	**понос**	*paNOS*
■ a fever	**температура**	*timpiraTUra*
■ a headache	**головная боль**	*galavNAya BOL'*
■ an infection	**инфекция**	*inFYEKtsiya*
■ a lump/swelling	**опухоль**	*Opukhal'*

◼ a sore throat   **ангина** *anGIna*

◼ a wound   **рана** *RAna*

I'm allergic to _____ .   **У меня аллергия от _____ .** *U miNYA alirGIya at*

◼ penicillin   **пеницилина** *pinitsiLIna*

I am taking this medicine.   **Я принимаю это лекарство.** *YA priniMAyu Eta liKARSTva*

I feel better.   **Я чувствую себя лучше.** *YA CHUSTvuyu siBYA LUCHshe*

I feel worse.   **Я чувствую себя хуже.** *YA CHUSTvuyu siBYA KHUzhe*

DOCTOR'S INSTRUCTIONS

Open your mouth!   **Откройте рот!** *atKROYtye ROT*

Stick out your tongue!   **Покажите язык!** *pakaZHYtye yiZYK*

Cough!   **Покашляйте!** *paKASHlyaytye*

Breathe deeply!   **Дышите глубоко!** *dySHYtye glubaKO*

Breathe normally!   **Дышите нормально!** *dySHYtye narMAL'na*

Undress (to the waist)!   **Разденьтесь (до пояса)!** *razDYEN'tis' (da POyasa)*

Lie down!   **Ложитесь!** *laZHYtis'*

Stand up!   **Вставайте!** *fstaVAYtye*

You may get dressed!   **Одевайтесь!** *adiVAYtis'*

PATIENT'S CONCERNS

Is it serious?   **Это серьёзно?** *Eta siR'YOZna*

Do I have to go to the hospital?   **Мне нужно лечь в больницу?** *MNYE NUZHna LYECH v bal'NItsu*

Are you giving me a prescription?	**Вы мне выпишете лекарство?** *VY MNYE VYpishitye liKARSTva*
How often should I take the medicine?	**Как часто принимать лекарство?** *KAK CHASta priniMAT' liKARSTva*
How long must I stay in bed?	**Сколько времени мне лежать?** *SKOL'ka VRYEmini MNYE liZHAT'*
Thank you for everything.	**Спасибо за всё.** *spaSIba za FSYO*

ACCIDENTS

Help!	**Помогите!** *pamaGItye*
Call a doctor!	**Вызовите врача!** *VYzavitye vraCHA*
Call an ambulance!	**Вызовите скорую помощь!** *VYzavitye SKOruyu POmash*
Take me to a hospital!	**Отвезите меня в больницу!** *atviZItye miNYA v bal'NItsu*
I fell.	**Я упал.** *YA uPAL*
I was knocked over.	**Меня сбили с ног.** *miNYA ZBIli s NOK*

I was hit by a car.	**Меня сбила машина.** *mINYA zbiLA maSHYna*
I'm having a heart attack.	**У меня сердечный приступ.** *u mINYA sirDYECHny PRIstup*
I burned myself.	**Я обварился.** *YA abvaRILsya*
I cut myself.	**Я порезался.** *YA paRYEzalsya*
I'm bleeding.	**У меня кровотечение.** *u miNYA kravatiCHEniye*
I've lost a lot of blood.	**Я потерял много крови.** *YA patiRYAL MNOga KROvi*
I think the bone is broken.	**Я думаю, у меня перелом.** *YA DUmayu u miNYA piriLOM*
The leg is swollen.	**Нога вздута.** *naGA VZDUta*
The wrist is twisted.	**Запястье растянуто.** *zaPYASt'ye raSTYAnuta*
My ankle is dislocated.	**Лодыжка вывыхнута.** *laDYSHka VYvykhnuta*

DENTIST

I have a terrible toothache.	**У меня страшно болит зуб.** *u miNYA STRASHna baLIT ZUP*
Where is the nearest dental clinic?	**Где ближайшая зубная поликлиника?** *GDYE bliZHAYshaya zubNAya paliKLInika*
I've lost a filling.	**Я потерял пломбу.** *YA patiRYAL PLOMbu*
I've broken a tooth.	**Я сломал зуб.** *YA slaMAL ZUP*
I can't chew.	**Я не могу жевать.** *YA NYE maGU zhiVAT'*
My gums hurt.	**Болят дёсны.** *baLYAT DYOSny*
Is there an infection?	**Это инфекция?** *Eta inFYEKtsiya*

Do you have to pull the tooth?	**Вам надо зуб удалить?** *VAM NAda ZUP udaLIT'*
Can you put in a filling?	**Можете поставить пломбу?** *MOzhitye paSTAvit' PLOMbu*
▪ an amalgam one	**амальгаму** *amal'GAmu*
▪ a gold one	**золотую** *zalaTUyu*
▪ a porcelain one	**фарфоровую** *farFOravuyu*
▪ a silver one	**серебряную** *siRYEbryanuyu*
▪ a temporary one	**временную** *VRYEminuyu*
Can you fix ____ ?	**Вы можете починить ____ ?** *VY MOzhitye pachiNIT'*
▪ this bridge	**этот мост** *Etat MOST*
▪ this crown	**эту коронку** *Etu kaRONku*
▪ my denture	**зубной протез** *zubNOY praTYES*
▪ this false tooth	**этот вставной зуб** *Etat fstavNOY ZUP*
When should I return?	**Когда мне вернуться?** *kagDA MNYE virNUtsa*
How much will it cost?	**Сколько это стоит?** *SKOL'ka Eta STOit*

OPTICIAN

Can you repair these glasses?	**Вы можете починить эти очки?** *VY MOzhitye pachiNIT' Eti achKI*
I've broken a lens.	**Я разбил стекло.** *YA razBIL stiKLO*
The frame broke.	**Разбилась оправа.** *razBIlas' aPRAva*
The arm is broken.	**Сломан заушник.** *SLOman zaUSHnik*
Can you put in a new lens?	**Можно вставить новое стекло?** *MOZHna FSTAvit' NOvaye stiKLO*

Can you tighten the screw?	**Можно подвернуть винтик?** *MOZHna padvirNUT' VINtik*
I need them urgently.	**Мне нужно срочно.** *MNYE NUZHna SROCHna*
I don't have an extra pair.	**У меня нет запасных.** *u miNYA NYET zapasNYKH*
Do you have contact lenses?	**У вас есть контактные линзы?** *u VAS YEST' kanTAKTniye LINzy*
Can you replace it immediately?	**Можете заменить сейчас?** *MOzhitye zamiNIT' siyCHAS*
Do you sell sunglasses?	**У вас продаются солнечные очки?** *u VAS pradaYUtsa SOLnichniye achKI*

TRAVEL TIP

Experienced travelers to Russia always carry a packet of tissues with them to use as napkins and to wipe their glasses, which fog up when going from the outdoor chill into the warmth of the Metro stations. In an emergency the tissues can substitute for toilet paper, sometimes in short supply. Other useful items are a pocket knife with screwdriver and corkscrew, plastic bags for wet clothes or shoes, a tube of spot remover, rubber bands, small packets of laundry detergent, a travel clothes-line, and a sink stopper.

COMMUNICATIONS

Most post offices are open from 9:00 AM to 6:00 PM with a one-hour break for lunch. The main post, telegraph, and telephone office on Tverskoy Street is open round the clock. Mail boxes are painted bright blue. Stamps are also available at many newsstands and kiosks. You might consider mailing home books that you receive as gifts: the cost is minimal, and you will be less burdened on the way home. In addition, you'll delight your friends with colorful, varied stamps from Russia. They make great collector's items.

POST OFFICE (ПОЧТА)

I want to mail a letter.	**Я хочу послать письмо.** *YA khaCHU paSLAT' piS'MO*
Where's a post office?	**Где почта?** *GDYE POCHta*
Where's the mailbox?	**Где почтовый ящик?** *GDYE pachTOvy YAshik*
What is the postage on ___ ?	**Сколько стоит ___ ?** *SKOL'ka STOit*
▨ a letter	**письмо** *piS'MO*
▨ an airmail letter	**авиаписьмо** *aviapiS'MO*
▨ an insured/certified letter	**ценное письмо** *TSEnaye piS'MO*
▨ a registered letter	**заказное письмо** *zakazNOye piS'MO*
▨ a special delivery letter	**письмо с доставкой** *piS'MO z daSTAFkay*
▨ a package	**посылка** *paSYLka*
▨ a postcard	**открытка** *atKRYTka*
▨ printed matter	**бандероль** *bandiROL'*
▨ to the USA	**в США** *f SA SHA A*
▨ to Canada	**в Канаду** *f kaNAdu*

▦ to Australia	**в Австралию** *v afSTRAliyu*
▦ to England	**в Англию** *v ANgliyu*

When will it arrive? (be received) **Когда получат?** *kagDA paLUchat*

Which window is for ____ ? **Какое окно за ____ ?** *kaKOye akNO za*

▦ general delivery	**до востребования** *da vasTRYEbavaniya*
▦ money order	**денежный перевод** *DYEnizhny piriVOT*
▦ stamps	**марки** *MARki*
▦ collector's stamps	**коллекционные марки** *kaliktsiOniye MARki*

Are there any letters for me? **Есть письма для меня?** *YEST' PIS'ma dlya miNYA*

My name is ____ . **Меня зовут ____ .** *miNYA zaVUT*

Please give me ____ . **Дайте мне, пожалуйста ____ .** *DAYtye MNYE paZHAlusta*

▦ ten postcards	**десять открыток** *DYEsit' atKRYtak*
▦ five 20-kopeck stamps	**пять марок по двадцать** *PYAT' MArak pa DVAtsat'*

TELEGRAMS (ТЕЛЕГРАММЫ)

Where do they accept telegrams? **Где принимают телеграммы?** *GDYE priniMAyut tiliGRAmy*

I want to send ____ . **Я хочу послать ____ .** *YA khaCHU paSLAT'*

▦ a fax	**телефакс** *tiliFAKS*
▦ a telegram	**срочную телеграмму** *SROCHnuyu tiliGRAmu*

▪ an international telegram	**международную телеграмму** *mizhdunaRODnuyu tiliGRAmu*
▪ a telex	**телекс** *TYEliks*
How much per word?	**Сколько стоит слово?** *SKOL'ka STOit SLOva*
Where are the forms?	**Где бланки?** *GDYE BLANki*
Can I send it collect?	**Можно послать доплатно?** *MOZHna paSLAT' daPLATna*
How long does a telegram take?	**Сколько времени идёт телеграмма?** *SKOL'ka VRYEmini iDYOT tiliGRama*

TELEPHONES (ТЕЛЕФОНЫ)

You usually can place local calls from your hotel room, either by dialing directly or by first dialing a single number for an outside line. For most calls within Russia you can also dial direct. For international calls you must place an order through the international operator or go to the General Post Office (**Главный Почтамт** *GLAVny pachTAMT*), where you also can call any location in Russia.

A local call from a telephone booth requires two kopecks. Some public phones accept 1-kopeck and 2-kopeck pieces, but others take only the 2-kopeck piece (**двушка** *DVUSHka*). You will not have a phone book in your room, but you may call Information (**05**) for the numbers of organizations, restaurants, embassies, and so forth. For private phone numbers, save the business cards that most professionals exchange at introductory meetings.

Where is ____ ?	**Где ____ ?** *GDYE*
▪ a pay telephone	**телефон-автомат** *tiliFON-aftaMAT*
▪ a telephone booth	**телефонная кабина** *tiliFOnaya kaBIna*
Can anyone change five kopecks?	**Кто может разменять пять копеек?** *KTO MOzhit razmiNYAT' PYAT' kaPYEyik*

I need a 2-kopeck piece.	**Мне нужна двушка.** *MNYE nuzhNA DVUSHka*
Can I use your phone?	**Можно от вас позвонить?** *MOZHna at VAS pazvaNIT'*
Here is the number.	**Вот номер.** *VOT NOmir*
Can you help me?	**Вы можете мне помочь?** *VY MOzhitye MNYE paMOCH*
I want to order ___ .	**Я хочу заказать ___ .** *YA khaCHU zakaZAT'*

- a long distance call **междугородный разговор** *mizhdugaRODny razgaVOR*
- an international call **международный разговор** *mizhdunaRODny razgaVOR*
- a person-to-person call **на человека** *na chilaVYEka*
- a station-to-station call **на номер** *na NOmir*

What is your telephone number?	**Какой у вас номер телефона?** *kaKOY u VAS NOmir tiliFOna*
And the area code?	**И код города?** *I KOT GOrada*
Operator, please dial this number for me.	**Девушка, набирайте, пожалуйста, этот номер.** *DYEvushka, nabiRAYtye paZHAlusta Etat NOmir*
I've been disconnected.	**Меня разъединили.** *miNYA razyidiNIli*
May I speak with ____ ?	**Можно говорить с ____ ?** *MOZHna gavaRIT' s*
I can barely hear you.	**Плохо слышно.** *PLOkha SLYSHna*
Speak louder!	**Говорите громче!** *gavaRItye GROMche*
Speak slowly!	**Говорите медленно!** *gavaRItye MYEDlina*
Who is speaking?	**Кто говорит?** *KTO gavaRIT*
Who is calling?	**Кто спрашивает?** *KTO SPRAshivayit*
Don't hang up!	**Не кладите трубку!** *NYE klaDItye TRUPku*
The line is busy.	**Занято.** *ZAnyata*
No one answers.	**Никто не подойдёт.** *niKTO NYE padaDYOT*
You've reached a wrong number.	**Вы не туда попали.** *VY NYE tuDA paPAli*
Call back later.	**Перезвоните позже.** *pirizvaNItye POzhe*
Please give him a message.	**Передайте ему, пожалуйста.** *piriDAYtye yiMU paZHAlusta*

DRIVING A CAR

   You may rent a car in Russia or drive your own car into the country. Check with Intourist on such matters as insurance and gas coupons. You should be familiar with European rules of the road and international road signs. Most major highways have signs in the Latin alphabet as well as Cyrillic, so you should have no trouble getting around. In major cities you generally are not permitted to make a left turn from major roadways unless there is a special left-turn lane. Instead, drive through the intersection, and after approximately fifty meters you can make a U-turn, after which you can turn right onto the desired street. This is called the **разворот**   *razvaROT*. Russians drive with their parking lights on in cities and use the headlights only outside city limits or on unlit stretches of road.

ROAD SIGNS

   Russia uses the international system of traffic signs. You should familiarize yourself with the important ones.

CAUTION SIGNS

Опасность
Caution

Скользкая дорога
Slippery Road

Пешеходный переход
Pedestrian Crossing

Опасный поворот
Dangerous Curve

Железнодорожный переезд
Railroad Crossing

REGULATION SIGNS

Главная дорога
Main Road

Уступите дорогу
Yield

Стоп
Stop

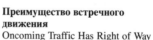

Преимущество встречного движения
Oncoming Traffic Has Right of Way

Въезд запрещён
No Entry

Движение запрещено
No Traffic

Разворот запрещён
No U-turn

Обгон запрещён
No Passing

Остановка запрещена
No Stopping

Стоянка запрещена
No Parking

Максимальная скорость
Maximum Speed

Конец ограничения
End of Restriction

PRESCRIPTIVE SIGNS

Минимальная скорость
Minimum Speed

Лёгковые автомобили
Cars Only

Пешеходная дорожка
Pedestrian Path

INFORMATION SIGNS

Место стоянки
Parking

Место для разворота
U-turn Permitted

Стоянка такси
Taxi Stand

Остановка трамвая
Trolley Stop

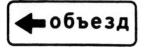

Объезд
Detour

Тупик
Dead End

Пост ГАИ
Traffic Police

PARKING

Parking in Russia does not pose a major problem, although along main streets you will notice a blue sign with a single red line for NO PARKING and with crossed red lines for NO STANDING.

CAR RENTALS

To reserve a car for rental, contact a travel bureau in advance. Otherwise you can rent a car in Russia. Rates vary according to the car you choose, and the charge for rental includes insurance. There is also a mileage charge. You need a valid driver's license.

I would like to rent _____ .	**Я хотел бы взять на прокат _____ .** *YA khaTYEL BY VZYAT' na praKAT*
a car	**машину** *maSHYnu*
a van	**микроавтобус** *mikraaFTObus*
with a driver	**с водителем** *s vaDItilim*
without a driver	**без водителя** *byez vaDItilya*
What kinds of cars do you have?	**Какие у вас машины?** *kaKIye u VAS maSHYny*
I prefer _____ .	**Я предпочитаю _____ .** *YA pritpachiTAyu*
a small car	**маленькую машину** *MAlin'kuyu maSHYnu*
a large car	**большую машину** *bal'SHUyu maSHYnu*
automatic transmission	**автоматическое переключение скоростей** *aftamaTIchiskaye piriklyuCHYEniye skaraSTYEY*
How much does it cost _____ ?	**Сколько она стоит _____ ?** *SKOL'ka aNA STOit*
per hour	**за час** *za CHAS*
per day	**за день** *za DYEN'*
per week	**за неделю** *za niDYElyu*
per month	**за месяц** *za MYEsits*
per kilometer	**за километр** *za kilaMYETR*
How much is the insurance?	**Сколько стоит страхование?** *SKOL'ka STOit strakhaVAniye*
Is gas included?	**Бензин входит в стоимость?** *binZIN FKHOdit f STOimast'*
Do you accept credit cards?	**Вы принимаете кредитные карточки?** *VY priniMAyitye kriDITniye KARtachki*
Here is my driver's license.	**Вот мои водительские права.** *VOT maYI vaDItil'skiye praVA*

Must I leave a deposit? **Мне нужно оставить залог?** *MNYE NUZHna aSTAvit' zaLOK*

What kind of gas does it take? **На каком бензине она работает?** *na kaKOM binZInye aNA raBOtayit*

ON THE ROAD

Excuse me! **Извините!** *izviNItye*

Can you tell me? **Вы не скажете?** *VY NYE SKAzhitye*

Where's the road to _____ ? **Где дорога в _____ ?** *GDYE daROga v*

Is this the road to _____ ? **Эта дорога в _____ ?** *Eta daROga v*

Where does this road go? **Куда идёт эта дорога?** *kuDA iDYOT Eta daROga*

How do I get to _____ ? **Как мне проехать в _____ ?** *KAK MNYE praYEkhat' v*

How many kilometers to _____ ? **Сколько километров до _____ ?** *SKOL'ka kilaMYEtraf da*

Do you have a road map? **У вас есть автодорожная карта?** *u VAS YEST' aftadaROZHnaya KARta*

Can you show me on the map?	**Вы можете мне показать на карте?** *VY MOzhitye MNYE pakaZAT' na KARtye*
In which direction should I go?	**В какое направление мне ехать?** *f kaKOye napravLYEniye MNYE YEkhat'*
Straight ahead?	**Прямо?** *PRYAma*
To the right?	**Направо?** *naPRAva*
To the left?	**Налево?** *naLYEva*
Where do I turn?	**Где мне повернуть?** *GDYE MNYE pavirNUT'*

AT THE SERVICE STATION

Gasoline is sold by the liter in Russia. You will need coupons (**талоны** *taLOny*), which can be purchased when you rent a vehicle. Credit is given for unused coupons. Most Europeans know approximately how many liters of gasoline they use per 100 kilometers. You may hear them say simply "ten liters," "eleven liters," and so on. To be safe, try to calculate your own mileage in the city and on the open road.

LIQUID MEASUREMENTS (APPROXIMATE)

LITERS	U.S. GALLONS	IMPERIAL GALLONS
30	8	6½
40	10½	8¾
50	13¼	11
60	15¾	13
70	18½	15½
80	21	17½

DISTANCE MEASURES (APPROXIMATE)

KILOMETERS	MILES
1	0.62
5	3
10	6
20	12
50	31
100	62

I'm running out of gas.	**Бензин у меня кончается.** *binZIN u miNYA kanCHAyitsa*
Where is the nearest service station?	**Где ближайшая бензоколонка?** *GDYE bliZHAYshaya binzakaLONka*
Twenty liters please _____ .	**Двадцать литров, пожалуйста _____ .** *DVAtsat' LItraf paZHAlusta*
▰ of regular (93 octane)	**девяносто третьего** *diviNOSta TRYEt'iva*
▰ of super (95 octane)	**девяносто пятого** *diviNOSta PYAtava*
Please check _____ .	**Проверьте, пожалуйста _____ .** *praVYER'tye paZHAlusta*
▰ the battery	**аккумулятор** *akumuLYAtar*
▰ the brakes	**тормоза** *tarmaZA*
▰ the carburetor	**карбюратор** *karbyuRAtar*
▰ the ignition sytem	**зажигание** *zazhiGAniye*
▰ the lights	**фары** *FAry*
▰ the oil	**масло** *MAsla*
▰ the spark plugs	**свечи** *SVYEchi*
▰ the tires	**шины** *SHYny*
▰ the water	**воду** *VOdu*
Can you _____ ?	**Вы можете _____ ?** *VY MOzhitye*
▰ charge the battery	**зарядить аккумулятор** *zariDIT' akumuLYAtar*

■ change the oil	**сменить масло**	*smiNIT' MAsla*
■ grease the car	**смазать машину**	*SMAzat' maSHYnu*
■ change the tire	**сменить колесо**	*smiNIT' kaliSO*

Where are the rest rooms?	**Где туалеты?** *GDYE tuaLYEty*

ACCIDENTS, REPAIRS

It overheats.	**Она перегревается.** *aNA pirigriVAyitsa*
It doesn't start.	**Она не заводится.** *aNA NYE zaVOditsa*
It doesn't go.	**Она не идёт.** *aNA NYE iDYOT*
I have a flat tire.	**У меня спустила шина.** *u miNYA spuSTIla SHYna*
The radiator is leaking.	**Радиатор протекает.** *radiAtar pratiKAyit*
The battery is dead.	**Аккумулятор сел.** *akumuLYAtar SYEL*
The keys are locked in the car.	**Ключи остались в машине.** *klyuCHI aSTAlis' v maSHYnye*
Is there a repair shop nearby?	**Поблизости есть автосервис?** *paBLIzasti YEST' aftaSYERvis*
Can you help me?	**Вы можете мне помочь?** *VY MOzhitye MNYE paMOCH*
Can you lend me _____ ?	**Можете одолжить _____ ?** *MOzhitye adalZHYT'*

■ a flashlight	**фонарь**	*faNAR'*
■ a hammer	**молоток**	*malaTOK*
■ a jack	**домкрат**	*damKRAT*
■ pliers	**плоскогубцы**	*plaskaGUPtsy*
■ a screwdriver	**отвёртку**	*atVYORTku*
■ a wrench	**гаечный ключ**	*GAyichny KLYUCH*

Do you have ____ ?	**У вас есть ____ ?** *u VAS YEST'*
◼ a bolt	**болт** *BOLT*
◼ a bulb	**лампочка** *LAMpachka*
◼ a filter	**фильтер** *FIL'tir*
◼ a nut	**гайка** *GAYka*

Can you fix the car?	**Можете машину починить?** *MOzhitye maSHYnu pachiNIT'*

Do you have this spare part?	**У вас есть эта запчасть?** *u VAS YEST' Eta zapCHAST'*

There's something wrong with ____ .	**Что-то не в порядке с ____ .** *SHTO-ta NYE f paRYATkye s*
◼ the directional signal	**сигнальным огнём** *sigNAL'nym agNYOM*
◼ the door handle	**ручкой** *RUCHkay*
◼ the electrical system	**электрической системой** *elikTRIchiskay siSTYEmay*
◼ the fan	**вентилятором** *vintiLYAtaram*
◼ the fan belt	**ремнём вентилятора** *rimNYOM vintiLYAtara*
◼ the fuel pump	**бензонасосом** *binzanaSOsam*
◼ the gears	**скоростями** *skaraSTYAmi*
◼ the gear shift	**сцеплением** *tsiPLYEniyim*
◼ the headlight	**фарой** *FAray*
◼ the horn	**гудком** *gutKOM*
◼ the ignition	**зажиганием** *zazhiGAniyim*
◼ the radio	**радио** *RAdio*
◼ the starter	**стартером** *STARtiram*
◼ the steering wheel	**рулём** *ruLYOM*
◼ the tail light	**задней фарой** *ZADnyey FAray*
◼ the transmission	**переключением скоростей** *piriklyuCHENiyim skaraSTYEY*

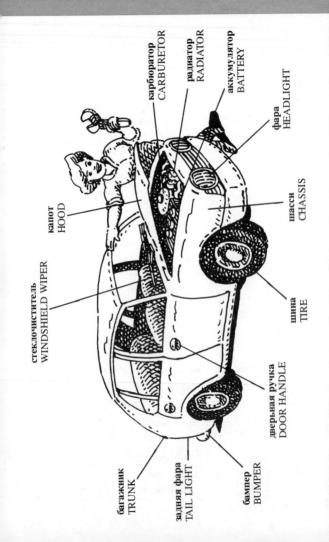

карбюратор CARBURETOR

радиатор RADIATOR

аккумулятор BATTERY

фара HEADLIGHT

шаси CHASSIS

капот HOOD

шина TIRE

стеклочиститель WINDSHIELD WIPER

дверная ручка DOOR HANDLE

багажник TRUNK

задняя фара TAIL LIGHT

бампер BUMPER

the water pump	водяным насосам	*vadiNYM naSOsam*
the windshield	ветровым стеклом	*vitraVYM stiKLOM*
Please look at ____ .	Посмотрите, пожалуйста ____ .	*pasmaTRItye paZHAlusta*
the brakes	тормоза	*tarmaZA*
the bumper	бампер	*BAMpir*
the exhaust	выхлопную трубку	*vykhlapNUyu TRUPku*
the fender	решётку	*riSHYOTku*
the gas tank	бензобак	*binzaBAK*
the hood	капот	*kaPOT*
the trunk	багажник	*baGAZHnik*
What's the matter?	В чём дело?	*F CHOM DYEla*
Can you do it today?	Можете сделать это сегодня?	*MOzhitye ZDYElat' Eta siVODnya*
How long (will it take)?	Как долго?	*KAK DOLga*
Is everything O.K.?	Всё в порядке?	*FSYO f paRYATkye*
How much do I owe you?	Сколько с меня?	*SKOL'ka s miNYA*

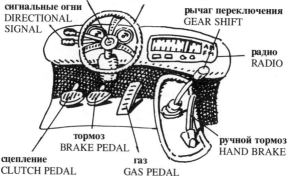

гудок HORN

рулевое колесо STEERING WHEEL

рычаг переключения GEAR SHIFT

сигнальные огни DIRECTIONAL SIGNAL

радио RADIO

тормоз BRAKE PEDAL

ручной тормоз HAND BRAKE

сцепление CLUTCH PEDAL

газ GAS PEDAL

GENERAL INFORMATION

Since Russians use the twenty-four hour clock, the PM hours are designated by the numbers thirteen to twenty.

TELLING TIME

What time is it?	**Который сейчас час?** *kaTOry siyCHAS CHAS*
One o'clock.	**Час.** *CHAS*
Two o'clock.	**Два часа.** *DVA chiSA*
Three o'clock.	**Три часа.** *TRI chiSA*
Four o'clock.	**Четыре часа.** *chiTYrye chiSA*
Five o'clock.	**Пять часов.** *PYAT' chiSOF*
Six o'clock.	**Шесть часов.** *SHEST' chiSOF*
Seven o'clock.	**Семь часов.** *SYEM' chiSOF*
Eight o'clock.	**Восемь часов.** *VOsim' chiSOF*
Nine o'clock.	**Девять часов.** *DYEvit' chiSOF*
Ten o'clock.	**Десять часов.** *DYEsit' chiSOF*
Eleven o'clock.	**Одиннадцать часов.** *aDInatsat' chiSOF*
Twelve o'clock.	**Двенадцать часов.** *dviNAtsat' chiSOF*
One o'clock PM.	**Тринадцать часов.** *triNAtsat' chiSOF*
Noon.	**Полдень.** *POLdyen'*
Midnight.	**Полночь.** *POLnach*

Once an hour has begun, Russians look forward to the next hour. Thus, 1:05 is "five minutes of the second hour."

1:05	**пять минут второго** *PYAT miNUT ftaROva*

2:10	**десять минут третьего** *DYEsit'* *miNUT TRYEt' yiva*
a quarter past three	**четверть четвёртого** *CHETvirt'* *chitVYORtava*
4:20	**двадцать минут пятого** *DVAtsat'* *miNUT PYAtava*
5:25	**двадцать пять минут шестого** *DVAtsat' PYAT" miNUT shiSTOva*
half past six	**половина седьмого** *palaVIna* *sid'MOva*

After the half hour Russians count backwards from the *next* hour; thus, 7:35 is eight minus twenty-five minutes.

7:35	**без двадцати пяти восемь** *byez* *dvatsaTI piTI VOsim'*
8:40	**без двадцати девять** *byez dvatsaTI* *DYEvit'*
9:45	**без четверти десять** *byes CHETvirti* *DYEsit'*
10:50	**без десяти одиннадцать** *byez disiTI* *aDInatsat'*
11:55	**без пяти двенадцать** *byes piTI* *dviNAtsat'*

EXPRESSIONS OF TIME

When?	**Когда?** *kagDA*
At what time?	**В котором часу?** *f kaTOram chiSU*
at five o'clock	**в пять часов** *f PYAT' chiSOF*
in an hour	**через час** *CHEris CHAS*
before two	**до двух** *da DVUKH*
after six	**после шести** *POslye shiSTI*
about seven	**около семи** *Okala siMI*
by eight	**к восьми** *k vas'MI*
From what time?	**С какого времени?** *s kaKOva VRYEmini*
Until what time?	**До какого времени?** *da kaKOva VRYEmini*
per hour	**за час** *za CHAS*
an hour ago	**час назад** *CHAS naZAT*
late	**поздно** *POZna*
early	**рано** *RAna*
on time	**вовремя** *VOvrimya*
in the morning	**утром** *Utram*
in the afternoon	**днём** *DNYOM*
in the evening	**вечером** *VYEchiram*
a second	**секунда** *siKUNda*
Just a minute!	**Минуточку!** *miNUtachku*
Right away!	**Сейчас!** *siyCHAS*

DAYS

What day is today?	**Какой сегодня день?** *kaKOY siVODnya DYEN'*

Today is _____ .	**Сегодня _____ .** *siVODnya*
▦ Monday	**понедельник** *paniDYEL'nik*
▦ Tuesday	**вторник** *FTORnik*
▦ Wednesday	**среда** *sriDA*
▦ Thursday	**четверг** *chitVERK*
▦ Friday	**пятница** *PYATnitsa*
▦ Saturday	**суббота** *suBOta*
▦ Sunday	**воскресенье** *vaskriSYEn'ye*
today	**сегодня** *siVODnya*
yesterday	**вчера** *fchiRA*
tomorrow	**завтра** *ZAFtra*
the day after tomorrow	**послезавтра** *pasliZAFtra*
the day before yesterday	**позавчера** *pazafchiRA*
on Wednesday	**в среду** *f SRYEdu*
a week from Tuesday	**во вторник через неделю** *va FTORnik CHEris niDYElyu*
a day	**день** *DYEN'*
a week	**неделя** *niDYElya*
a month	**месяц** *MYEsits*
a year	**год** *GOT*
a working day	**рабочий день** *raBOchi DYEN'*
a day off	**выходной день** *vykhadNOY DYEN'*
a holiday	**праздник** *PRAZnik*

MONTHS

January	**январь** *yanVAR'*
February	**февраль** *fiVRAL'*
March	**март** *MART*

April	**апрель** *aPRYEL'*
May	**май** *MAY*
June	**июнь** *iYUN'*
July	**июль** *iYUL'*
August	**август** *AVgust*
September	**сентябрь** *sinTYABR'*
October	**октябрь** *akTYABR'*
November	**ноябрь** *naYABR'*
December	**декабрь** *diKABR'*

DATES

What's today's date?	**Какое сегодня число?** *kaKOye siVODnya chiSLO*
The fifth of May.	**Пятое мая.** *PYAtaye MAya*
When did it happen?	**Когда это случилось?** *kagDA Eta sluCHIlas'*
On June 1, 1991.	**Первого июня, девяноста первого года.** *PYERvava iYUnya diviNOSta PYERvava GOda*

SEASONS

in the spring	**весной** *viSNOY*
in the summer	**летом** *LYEtam*
in the fall	**осенью** *Osin'yu*
in the winter	**зимой** *ziMOY*
every summer	**каждое лето** *KAZHdaye LYEta*
last year	**в прошлом году** *f PROSHlam gaDU*
next year	**в будущем году** *v BUdushim gaDU*

WEATHER

How is the weather today?	**Какая сегодня погода?** *kaKAya siVODnya paGOda*
The weather today is ___ .	**Сегодня погода ___ .** *siVODnya paGOda*
■ good	**хорошая** *khaROshaya*
■ bad	**плохая** *plaKHAya*
What splendid weather!	**Какая прекрасная погода!** *kaKAya priKRASnaya paGOda*
Today it's ___ .	**Сегодня ___ .** *siVODnya*
■ hot	**жарко** *ZHARka*
■ warm	**тепло** *tiPLO*
■ cold	**холодно** *KHOladna*
■ cool	**прохладно** *praKHLADna*
The sun is shining.	**Светит солнце.** *SVYEtit SONtsa*
The wind is blowing.	**Дует ветер.** *DUyit VYEtir*
It's raining.	**Идёт дождь.** *iDYOT DOSH*
It's snowing.	**Идёт снег.** *iDYOT SNYEK*

TEMPERATURE CONVERSIONS

To change degrees Fahrenheit to Centigrade, subtract 32 and multiply by $^5/_9$.

$$41°F - 32 = 9 \times {}^5/_9 = 5°C$$

To convert from Centigrade to Fahrenheit, multiply by $^9/_5$ and add 32

$$10°C \times {}^9/_5 = 18 + 32 = 50°F$$

To get an approximate temperature quickly, take the degrees Fahrenheit, subtract 30 and divide by 2, or, take the degrees Centigrade, multiply by 2, and add 30.

Most seasoned travelers know a few temperatures for reference.

DEGREES	
Fahrenheit	Celsius
212	100
98.6	37
86	30
77	25
68	20
50	10
32	0
14	− 10
− 4	− 20
− 22	− 30
− 40	− 40

It is small consolation that at minus 40 degrees, Fahrenheit and Centigrade temperatures are identical.

OFFICIAL HOLIDAYS

January 1—New Year's Day · **1 января** **Новый год**

March 8—International Women's Day · **8 марта** **Международный женский день**

May 1—May Day Worker's Day · **1 мая** **Первое мая**

May 9—Victory Day · **9 мая** **День победы**

October 7—Constitution Day · **7 октября** **День конституции**

November 7— Anniversary of the Great October Socialist Revolution	**7 ноября Годовщина Великой Октябрьской Социалистической Революции**
Happy Birthday!	**С днём рождения!** *z DNYOM raZHDYEniya*
Happy holiday!	**С праздником!** *s PRAZnikam*
Happy New Year!	**С Новым годом!** *s NOvym GOdam*

The Russian Orthodox Church still observes Christmas and Easter according to the pre-revolutionary calendar.

Merry Christmas! (with the birth of Christ)	**С рождеством Христовым!** *s razhdiSTVOM khriSTOvym*
Happy Easter! (Christ is risen)	**Христос воскресе!** *khriSTOS vaSKRYEs'ye*

FORMER SOVIET REPUBLICS AND CAPITALS

At the beginning of 1991, there were fifteen republics in the Soviet Union. In official documents and lists you will often encounter their abbreviations, in which the final three letters **ССР** stand for **Советская Социалистическая Республика** *saVYETskaya satsialiSTIchiskaya risPUblika* —Soviet Socialist Republic. The exception is the Russian Soviet Federated Socialist Republic—**РСФСР** *RSFSR*. The official name of the country was **Союз Советских Социалистических Республик** *saYUS saVYETskikh satsialiSTIchiskikh risPUblik* (Union of Soviet Socialist Republics), abbreviated as **СССР** *SSSR*, with the capital in Moscow—**Москва** *maskVA*.

Armenia (capital, Yerevan)	**Армения (Ереван)**
Azerbaijan (Baky)	**Азербайджан (Баку)**
Belarus (Mensk)	**Беларусь (Минск)**
Estonia (Tallinn)	**Эстония (Таллинн)**
Georgia (Tbilisi)	**Грузия (Тбилиси)**
Kazakhstan (Almaty)	**Казахстан (Алма-Ата)**

Kyrgyzstan (Bishkek)	**Кыргызстан (Бишкек)**
Latvia (Riga)	**Латвия (Рига)**
Lithuania (Vilnius)	**Литва (Вильнюс)**
Moldova (Chisinau)	**Молдова (Кишинёв)**
Russia (Moscow)	**Россия (Москва)**
Tajikistan (Dushanbe)	**Таджикистан (Душанбе)**
Turkmenistan (Ashgabat)	**Туркменистан (Ашхабад)**
Ukraine (Kiev)	**Украина (Киев)**
Uzbekistan (Toshkent)	**Узбекистан (Ташкент)**

At the beginning of 1991, the Soviet Union had almost two hundred nationalities. All people were Soviet citizens (**советский гражданин** *saVYETski grazhdaNIN*), but they normally identified themselves by nationality.

I'm a Russian.	**Я русский.** (*m*) *YA RUski*
	Я русская. (*f*) *YA RUskaya*
I'm an Estonian.	**Я эстонец.** (*m*) *YA eSTOnits*
	Я эстонка. (*f*) *YA eSTONka*
I'm a Ukrainian.	**Я украинец.** (*m*) *YA ukraInits*
	Я украинка. (*f*) *YA ukraINka*

Using the same principles, you can identify yourself.

I'm American.	**Я американец.** (*m*) *YA amiriKAnits*
	Я американка. (*f*) *YA amiriKANka*
I'm Australian.	**Я австралиец.** (*m*) *YA afstraLIyits*
	Я австралийка. (*f*) *YA afstraLIYka*
I'm British.	**Я англичанин.** (*m*) *YA angliCHAnin*
	Я англичанка. (*f*) *YA angliCHANka*
I'm Canadian.	**Я канадец.** (*m*) *YA kaNAdits*
	Я канадка. (*f*) *YA kaNATka*

COUNTRIES AND NATIONALITIES

Where are you from?	**Откуда вы?**	*otKUda VY*
I'm from ____ (plus genitive case).	**Я из ____ .**	*YA IS*
Africa	**Африка**	*AFrika*
Asia	**Азия**	*Aziya*
Australia	**Австралия**	*afSTRAliya*
Europe	**Европа**	*yiVROpa*
America	**Америка**	*aMYErika*
Austria	**Австрия**	*AFstriya*
Belgium	**Бельгия**	*BYEL'giya*
Canada	**Канада**	*KaNAda*
China	**Китай**	*KiTAY*
England	**Англия**	*ANgliya*
France	**Франция**	*FRANtsiya*
Germany	**Германия**	*girMAniya*
Greece	**Греция**	*GRYEtsiya*
Hungary	**Венгрия**	*VYENgriya*
India	**Индия**	*INdiya*
Ireland	**Ирландия**	*irLANdiya*
Israel	**Израиль**	*izraIL'*
Italy	**Италия**	*iTAliya*
Japan	**Япония**	*yaPOniya*
Norway	**Норвегия**	*narVYEgiya*
Poland	**Польша**	*POL'sha*
Portugal	**Португалия**	*partuGAliya*
Scotland	**Шотландия**	*shatLANdiya*
the Soviet Union	**Советский Союз**	*saVYETsky saYUS*

Spain	**Испания** *iSPAniya*
Sweden	**Швеция** *SHVEtsiya*
Switzerland	**Швейцария** *shviyTSAriya*
the United States	**Соединённые Штаты** *sayidiNYOniye SHTAty*

DIRECTIONS

north	**север** *SYEvir*
south	**юг** *YUK*
east	**восток** *vaSTOK*
west	**запад** *ZApat*

IMPORTANT SIGNS

Up	**Вверх** *VVYERKH*
Down	**Вниз** *VNIS*
Entrance	**Вход** *FKHOT*
Exit	**Выход** *VYkhat*
Women	**Женщины** *ZHENshiny*
Reserved	**Заказано** *zaKAzana*
Closed	**Закрыто** *zaKRYta*
Occupied	**Занято** *ZAnita*
Emergency Exit	**Запасный выход** *zaPASny VYkhat*
Go	**Идите** *iDItye*
Pull	**К себе** *k siBYE*
Cashier	**Касса** *KAsa*
Elevator	**Лифт** *LIFT*

No Vacancies (no places)	**Мест нет** *MYEST NYET*
Men	**Мужчины** *mushCHIny*
No Smoking	**Не курить** *NYE kuRIT'*
Don't Touch	**Не трогать** *NYE TROgat'*
Bus Stop	**Остановка автобуса** *astaNOFka aFTObusa*
Caution	**Осторожно** *astaROZHna*
Push	**От себя** *at siBYA*
Open	**Открыто** *atKRYta*
On Break	**Перерыв** *piriRYF*
Wait	**Стойте** *STOYtye*
Toilet	**Туалет** *tuaLYET*

ABBREVIATIONS

ан	**Академия Наук** Academy of Sciences
АЭС	**атомная электростанция** atomic power station
ВДНХ	**Выставка достижений народного хозяйства** Exhibition of Achievements of the National Economy
ГАИ	**Государственная автомобильная инспекция** State Automobile Inspection
ГУМ	**Государственный универсальный магазин** State Department Store
ГЭС	**гидроэлектрическая станция** hydroelectric station
ин.	**иностранный** foreign
и т.д.	**и так далее** et cetera (etc.)
и т.п.	**и тому подобное** and so forth

к.	**копейка** kopeck
КГБ	**Комитет государственной безопасности** Committee for State Security
кг.	**килограмм** kilogram
КП	**Коммунистическая партия** Communist Party
гр.	**гражданин** (*m*) citizen
гр-ка	**гражданка** (*f*) citizen
МГУ	**Московский государственный университет** Moscow State University
мл.	**младший** junior
мм.	**миллиметр** millimeter
р.	**рубль** ruble
СССР	USSR
ст.	**старший** senior
ст.	**станция** station
стр.	**страница** page
США	USA
ТАСС	**Телеграфное агенство Советского Союза** TASS—Wire Agency of the Soviet Union
ц.	**цена** price
ЦК	**Центральный Комитет** Central Committee
ч.	**час** o'clock
шт.	**штука** an item

METRIC CONVERSIONS

If you are not used to the metric system, you'll need the following tables and conversion charts during your visit to Russia.

SOME CONVENIENT ROUGH EQUIVALENTS

These are rough approximations, but they'll help you to "think metric" when you don't have a pocket calculator handy.

3 километра (kilometers)	= 2 miles
30 грамм (grams)	= 1 ounce
100 грамм (grams)	= 3.5 ounces
1 килограмм (kilogram)	= 2 pounds
1 литр (liter)	= 1 quart
1 гектар (hectare)	= 1 acre

CENTIMETERS/INCHES

It is usually unnecessary to make exact conversions from inches to the metric system, but to give you an approximate idea of how they compare, we give the following guide.

To convert **сантиметры** *santiMYEtry* (centimeters) to **дюймы** *DYUYmy* (inches), multiply by 0.39.

To convert inches (**дюймы**) to centimeters (**сантиметры**), multiply by 2.54.

Сантиметры

Дюймы

METERS/FEET

1 метр (meter)= **39.37 дюймов** (inches)
1 фут (foot)= **0.3 метр** (meter)
1 метр (meter)= **3.28 фута** (feet)
1 ярд (yard)= **0.9 метр** (meter)
1 метр (meter)= **1.09 ярд** (yard)

How tall are you in meters? See for yourself.

Футы/Дюймы (Feet/Inches)	Метры/Сантиметры (Meters/Centimeters)
5	1.52
5 1	1.545
5 2	1.57
5 3	1.595
5 4	1.62
5 5	1.645
5 6	1.68
5 7	1.705
5 8	1.73
5 9	1.755
5 10	1.78
5 11	1.805
6	1.83
6 1	1.855

WHEN YOU WEIGH YOURSELF

1 килограмм (kilogram) = **2.2 фунта** (pounds)
1 фунт (pound) = **0.45 килограмма** (kilogram)

Килограммы KILOGRAMS	Фунты POUNDS
40	88
45	99
50	110
55	121
60	132
65	143
70	154
75	165
80	176
85	187
90	198
95	209
100	220

LIQUID MEASUREMENTS

1 литр (liter) = **1.06 кварта** (quart)
4 литра (liters) = **1.06 галлон** (gallon)

For quick approximate conversion, multiply the number of gallons (**галлоны**) by 4 to get liters (**литры**). Divide the number of **литры** (liters) by 4 to get **галлоны** (gallons).

EMERGENCY TELEPHONE NUMBERS

Fire	**Пожарная охрана**	**01**
Police	**Милиция**	**02**
Medical care	**Скорая помощь**	**03**
Gas leaks	**Газ**	**04**

MINI-DICTIONARY FOR BUSINESS TRAVELERS

amount	**сумма**	*SUma*
appraise	**оценивать**	*aTSEnivat'*
authorize	**уполномочивать**	*upalnaMOchivat'*
authorized edition	**авторизованное издание**	*avtariZOvanaye izDAniye*
bill	**счёт**	*SHOT*
bill of exchange	**вексель**	*VYEKsil'*
bill of lading	**коносамент**	*kanasaMYENT*
bill of sale	**товарный чек**	*taVARny CHEK*
business operation	**дело**	*DYEla*
cash payment	**наличный расчёт**	*naLICHny raSHOT*
buy	**купить**	*kuPIT'*
cash a check	**получить деньги по чеку**	*paluCHIT' DYEN' gi pa CHEku*
certified check	**расчётный чек**	*raSHOTny CHEK*

chamber of commerce	**торговая палата** *tarGOvaya paLAta*
compensation for damages	**возмещение убытков** *vazmiSHEniye uBYTkaf*
competition	**конкуренция** *kankuRYENtsiya*
competitive price	**конкурентоспособная цена** *kankurintaspaSOBnaya tsiNA*
contract	**контракт** *kanTRAKT*
contractual obligations	**контрактные обязательства** *kanTRAKTniye abiZAtil'stva*
controlling interest	**контрольный пакет акций** *kanTROL'ny paKYET AKtsi*
co-owner	**совладелец** *savlaDYElits*
co-partner	**партнёр** *partNYOR*
delivery	**поставка** *paSTAFka*
down payment	**первоначальный платёж** *pirvanaCHAL'ny plaTYOSH*
(payment) due	**подлежит оплате** *padliZHYT' aPLAtye*
enterprise	**предприятие** *pritpriYAtiye*
expedite delivery	**продвинуть поставку** *praDVInut' paSTAFku*
expenses	**затраты / расходы** *zaTRAty / rasKHOdy*
goods	**товары** *taVAry*
hard currency	**валюта** *vaLYUta*
infringement of patent rights	**нарушение патентных прав** *naruSHEniye paTYENTnykh PRAF*
insurance	**страхование** *strakhaVAniye*
international law	**международное право** *mizhdunaRODnaye PRAva*
lawful possessions	**законное имущество** *zaKOnaye iMUshistva*

lawsuit	**судебный процесс** *suDYEBny praTSES*
lawyer	**адвокат** *advaKAT*
letter of credit	**аккредитив** *akridiTIF*
mail-order business	**посылочная фирма** *paSYlachnaya FIRma*
manager	**директор / заведующий** *diRYEKtar / zaVYEdushi*
market value (price)	**рыночная цена** *RYnachnaya tsiNA*
payment	**платёж** *plaTYOSH*
partial payment	**частичный платёж** *chiSTICHny plaTYOSH*
installment	**рассрочка** *raSROCHka*
overdue	**просроченный** *praSROchiny*
price	**цена** *tsiNA*
retail price	**розничная цена** *ROZnichnaya tsiNA*
property	**имущество** *iMUshistva*
purchasing agent	**покупательный агент** *pakuPAtil'ny aGYENT*
put on the market	**поставить на рынок** *paSTAvit' na RYnak*
sale	**продажа** *praDAzha*
to sell	**продавать** *pradaVAT'*
to send	**послать** *paSLAT'*
to send back	**возвращать** *vazvraSHAT'*
to send COD	**послать наложенным платежом** *paSLAT' naLOzhinym platiZHOM*
shipment	**отправка / отгрузка** *atPRAFka / adGRUSka*
tax	**налог** *naLOK*
tax-exempt	**освобождённый от налогов** *asvabazhDYOny at naLOgaf*

sales tax	**налог на покупки** *naLOK na paKUPki*
trade	**торговля** *tarGOvlya*
transact business	**вести дела** *viSTI diLA*
transfer	**перевод** *piriVOT*
transportation charges	**плата на транспорт / на перевозку** *PLAta na TRANSpart / na piriVOSku*
via	**через** *CHEris*
yield a profit	**приносить прибыль** *prinaSIT' PRIbyl'*

TRAVEL TIP

Russia is not the place to show off your new wardrobe. Often you will be wrapped in a warm overcoat. Why not take along some well-worn items that you are tired of and planning to part with anyway? Before departure you can leave the items with the maid or "key lady," who will find good use for them. This way you save on laundry and make some room for the souvenirs that you are bound to accumulate during the trip.

QUICK GRAMMAR GUIDE

Russian is an inflected language. Nouns, pronouns, modifiers, and verbs change their forms to convey different meanings. Normally, the lexical meaning of the word is in the root, the beginning part of a word. The grammatical meaning is contained in the different endings.

NOUNS

Russian nouns are classed according to their gender, number, and case. They can be masculine, feminine, or neuter. Gender is a grammatical category not necessarily coinciding with biological reality. Masculine nouns usually end in a consonant. Feminine nouns often end in **-a** or **-я**. Neuter nouns generally end in **-o** or **-e**.

Russian nouns can be singular or plural in each of the six cases: nominative, accusative, genitive, prepositional, dative, and instrumental. (Tip: It suffices in most situations to know the nominative and accusative cases).

MASCULINE NOUNS

SINGULAR	HARD CONSONANTS	SOFT CONSONANTS
Nominative	журнал	портфель
Accusative	журнал	портфель
Genitive	журнала	портфеля
Prepositional	журнале	портфеле
Dative	журналу	портфелю
Instrumental	журналом	портфелем
PLURAL		
Nominative	журналы	портфели
Accusative	журналы	портфели
Genitive	журналов	портфелей
Prepositional	журналах	портфелях
Dative	журналам	портфелям
Instrumental	журналами	портфелями

NEUTER NOUNS

SINGULAR	ENDING IN -o	ENDING IN -e
Nominative	письмо	здание
Accusative	письмо	здание
Genitive	письма	здания
Prepositional	письме	здании
Dative	письму	зданию
Instrumental	письмом	зданием

PLURAL		
Nominative	письма	здания
Accusative	письма	здания
Genitive	писем	зданий
Prepositional	письмах	зданиях
Dative	письмам	зданиям
Instrumental	письмами	зданиями

FEMININE NOUNS

SINGULAR	ENDING IN -a	ENDING IN -я
Nominative	телеграмма	тётя
Accusative	телеграмму	тётю
Genitive	телеграммы	тёти
Prepositional	телеграмме	тёте
Dative	телеграмме	тёте
Instrumental	телеграммой	тётей

PLURAL		
Nominative	телеграммы	тёти
Accusative	телеграммы	тётей
Genitive	телеграмм	тётей
Prepositional	телеграммах	тётях
Dative	телеграммам	тётям
Instrumental	телеграммами	тётями

Some Russian feminine nouns end in the soft sign **-ь**, and a few neuter nouns end in **-я**. In both instances the nominative and accusative cases are identical. You may see some variations of the above endings caused by spelling rules in Russian. The three key rules are

"8" rule: After these eight letters (**г, к, х, ж, ч, ш, щ, ц**) you may not write the letters **я** or **ю**, but must replace them with **a** or **y**.

"7" rule: After these seven letters (**г, к, х, ж, ч, ш, щ**) you may not write the letter **ы**, but must write **и**.

"5" rule: After these five letters (**ж, ч, ш, щ, ц**) you may write the letter **о** only if it is accented. When it is not accented, you replace the expected **о** with the letter **е**.

PRONOUNS

Pronouns replace, or stand in for, nouns. They also have gender, number, and case. The following personal pronouns are important for travelers.

Singular	I	you	he (it)	she
Nom.	**я**	**ты**	**он (оно)**	**она**
Acc.	**меня**	**тебя**	**его**	**её**
Gen.	**меня**	**тебя**	**его**	**её**
Prep.	**мне**	**тебе**	**нём**	**ней**
Dat.	**мне**	**тебе**	**ему**	**ей**
Instr.	**мной**	**тобой**	**им**	**ей**

Plural	we	you	they
Nom.	**мы**	**вы**	**они**
Acc.	**нас**	**вас**	**их**
Gen.	**нас**	**вас**	**их**
Prep.	**нас**	**вас**	**них**
Dat.	**нам**	**вам**	**им**
Instr.	**нами**	**вами**	**ими**

	who?	what?
Nom.	**кто**	**что**
Acc.	**кого**	**что**
Gen.	**кого**	**чего**
Prep.	**ком**	**чём**
Dat.	**кому**	**чему**
Instr.	**кем**	**чем**

ADJECTIVES/POSSESSIVE MODIFIERS

Modifiers in Russian agree with the noun in gender, number, and case. Knowing the spelling rule will help you figure out these endings. (Hint: When the ending of the noun changes, the ending of the modifier is also likely to change.)

	SINGULAR			PLURAL
	Masculine	Neuter	Feminine	All Genders
Nom.	новый	новое	новая	новые
Acc.	новый	новое	новую	новые
Gen.	нового	нового	новой	новых
Prep.	новом	новом	новой	новых
Dat.	новому	новому	новой	новым
Instr.	новым	новым	новой	новыми
Nom.	мой	моё	моя	мои
Acc.	мой	моё	мою	мои
Gen.	моего	моего	моей	моих
Prep.	моём	моём	моей	моих
Dat.	моему	моему	моей	моим
Instr.	моим	моим	моей	моими
Nom.	наш	наше	наша	наши
Acc.	наш	наше	нашу	наши
Gen.	нашего	нашего	нашей	наших
Prep.	нашем	нашем	нашей	наших
Dat.	нашему	нашему	нашей	нашим
Instr.	нашим	нашим	нашей	нашими

ADVERBS

Russian adverbs do not change their form. Most are readily identifiable by the endings **-o/-e** or **-и**. Some examples are

quickly	**быстро**
slowly	**медленно**
of course	**конечно**
automatically	**автоматически**

To make the comparative adverbs (quicker, slower, etc.) you change the **-o** into **-ee**

quicker	**быстрее**
slower	**медленнее**

To make the comparative of adverbs ending in **-и** you add **более** (more) or **менее** (less) before the word.

more automatically	**более автоматически**
less practically	**менее практически**

VERBS

The dictionary form of most verbs (the infinitive) ends in **-ть**. All Russian verbs have aspect, a grammatical category rendered in other ways in English. Russian aspect can be perfective or imperfective and reflects a Russian's way of looking at the world.

THE PAST TENSE

The past tense is formed by replacing the **-ть** of the infinitive form with **-л** for the masculine singular or adding **-ла** for the feminine singular, **-ло** for the neuter singular, or **-ли** for all plurals.

to sell	**продавать**
I was selling.	**Я продавал.**
Masha was selling.	**Маша продавала.**
We, You, They sold.	**Мы, Вы, Они продавали.**

to buy	**купить**
Ivan bought.	**Иван купил.**
Irina bought.	**Ирина купила.**
We, You, They bought.	**Мы, Вы, Они купили.**

IMPERFECTIVE PRESENT/PERFECTIVE FUTURE

Russian verbs belong to one of two conjugations (verb classes). The final consonants in both conjugations are the same: only the vowels **e** or **и** change to indicate that a verb belongs to the first or second conjugation. If the verb is imperfective, the conjugated form is in the present tense. The conjugated form of a perfective verb signifies the future.

First Conjugation		Second Conjugation	
to work	**работать**	to speak with	**поговорить**
I work.	**Я работаю.**	I'll speak.	**Я поговорю.**
You work.	**Ты работаешь.**	You'll speak.	**Ты поговоришь.**
He works.	**Он работает.**	She'll speak	**Она поговорит.**
We work.	**Мы работаем.**	We'll speak.	**Мы поговорим.**
You work.	**Вы работаете.**	You'll speak.	**Вы поговорите.**
They work.	**Они работают.**	They'll speak.	**Они поговорят.**

THE IMPERFECTIVE FUTURE

To form the future of imperfective verbs, add the future forms of the verb "to be" **быть** to the imperfective infinitive.

to be	**быть**	to work	**работать**
I will be	**я буду**	I will be working.	**Я буду работать.**
you will be	**ты будешь**	You will be working.	**Ты будешь работать.**
she will be	**она будет**	He will be working.	**Он будет работать.**
we will be	**мы будем**	We will be working.	**Мы будем работать.**
you will be	**вы будете**	You will be working.	**Вы будете работать.**
they will be	**они будут**	They will be working.	**Они будут работать.**

COMMANDS

Most commands will be easily identifiable. Almost all have the ending **-айте/-яйте** or **-ите**.

Listen!	**Слушайте!**
Repeat!	**Повторяйте!**
Look!	**Смотрите!**
Help!	**Помогите!**
Go away!	**Отойдите!**

QUESTIONS

Most questions in Russian can be formed by using one of the interrogative pronouns (question words).

Who?	**Кто?**	*KTO*
What?	**Что?**	*SHTO*
Where?	**Где?**	*GDYE*
Where to?	**Куда?**	*kuDA*
When?	**Когда?**	*kagDA*

Why?	**Почему?**	*pachiMU*
How?	**Как?**	*KAK*
How much?	**Сколько?**	*SKOL'ka*

In a sentence without an interrogative, Russians use a rising tone on the word in question.

| Are you working on Saturday? | **Вы работаете в субботу?** |
| Do you want to go? | **Вы хотите пойти?** |

NEGATIONS

Form the negative by placing **не** before the verb or any other word you wish to negate.

| I don't speak Ukrainian. | **Я не говорю по-украински.** |
| No, not that one. | **Нет, не это.** |

You can always use the famous Russian "NO"—**НЕТ** for emphasis.

WORD ORDER

In general, Russian word order is freer than English. A basic rule is that any new information and consequently the most important facts are found at the end of the sentence.

PREPOSITIONS

Most prepositions are not accented in speech but are pronounced together with the following word. The list below should be helpful.

about	**о**	*a*
according to	**по**	*pa*
across	**через**	*CHEris*
after	**после**	*POslye*
among	**среди**	*sriDI*
around	**вокруг**	*vaKRUK*
at	**у**	*u*
before	**до / перед**	*da / PYErit*

behind	**за**	*za*
between	**между**	*MYEZHdu*
down	**вниз**	*VNIS*
during	**во время**	*va VRYEmya*
except	**кроме**	*KROmye*
for	**для**	*dlya*
from	**из / с / от**	*is / s / at*
in	**в**	*v*
in front of	**перед**	*PYErit*
inside	**внутри**	*vnuTRI*
on	**на**	*na*
on top	**над**	*nat*
opposite	**напротив**	*naPROtif*
outside	**вне**	*vnye*
through	**через**	*CHEris*
to	**в / на**	*v / na*
toward	**к**	*k*
under	**под**	*pat*
until	**до**	*da*
with	**с**	*s*
without	**без**	*byes*

TRAVEL TIP

Russians love winter and impatiently await its arrival. Dress warmly and wear waterproof shoes or boots, because the distances between buildings are great, and the streets and sidewalks tend to be slushy from October through May. You might purchase a fur hat with ear flaps (**ушанка** *uSHANka*) as a practical addition to your wardrobe and a great souvenir of your visit.

READY
REFERENCE KEY

Here are some phrases and words from the book that you are likely to use often. For a more extensive list of phrases, refer to the appropriate chapter in the book.

SIMPLE WORDS AND PHRASES

Do you speak English?	**Вы говорите по-английски?** *VY gavaRItye pa-anGLIYski*
I speak a little Russian.	**Я говорю немного по-русски.** *YA gavaRYU niMNOga pa-RUski*
Do you understand?	**Вы понимаете?** *VY paniMAyitye*
I understand.	**Я понимаю.** *YA paniMAyu*
I don't understand.	**Я не понимаю.** *YA NYE paniMAyu*
How do you say ___ in Russian?	**Как ___ по-русски?** *KAK pa-RUski*
Please repeat.	**Повторите, пожалуйста.** *paftaRItye paZHAlusta.*

BEING POLITE

Hello.	**Здравствуйте.** *ZDRASTvuytye*
Yes.	**Да.** *DA*
No.	**Нет.** *NYET*
Please.	**Пожалуйста.** *paZHAlusta*
Thank you.	**Спасибо.** *spaSIba*
Excuse me!	**Извините!** *izviNItye*
That's all right.	**Хорошо.** *kharaSHO*

| It doesn't matter. | **Ничего.** *nichiVO* |
| Goodbye. | **До свидания.** *da sviDAniya* |

BASIC NEEDS

What is it?	**Что это?** *SHTO Eta*
When?	**Когда?** *kagDA*
Where?	**Где?** *GDYE*
Where to?	**Куда?** *kuDA*
▮ to the right	**направо** *naPRAva*
▮ to the left	**налево** *naLYEva*
▮ straight ahead	**прямо** *PRYAma*
How much does it cost?	**Сколько стоит?** *SKOL'ka STOit*
I'd like ____ .	**Мне хочется** ____ . *MNYE KHOchitsa*
Please bring me ____ .	**Принесите мне, пожалуйста** ____ . *priniSItye MNYE paZHAlusta*
Please show me ____ .	**Покажите мне, пожалуйста** ____ . *pakaZHYtye MNYE paZHAlusta*

ENGLISH—RUSSIAN DICTIONARY

Accented syllables are indicated by capital letters in the italicized phonetic transcription. Verbs are identified according to their aspects: (*i*) imperfective; (*p*) perfective. Nouns that end in the soft sign "**ъ**" are either (*m*) masculine or (*f*) feminine; neuter nouns that do not end in **o** or **e** are indicated by an (*n*). All definitions reflect only the usage(s) actually presented in the chapters of this book.

A

abdomen живот *zhiVOT*

able мочь (*i*) *MOCH*

about о / об *O / OP*

above над *NAT*

abscess нарыв *naRYF*

accept принимать (*i*) *priniMAT'*

accepted, acceptable принято *PRInita*

according to по *PO*

account счёт *SHOT*

accumulate набраться (*p*) *naBRAtsa*

ace (cards) туз *TUS*

achievement достижение *dastiZHEniye*

get acquainted познакомиться (*p*) *paznaKOmitsa*

across через *CHEris*

active действующий *DYEYSTvuyushi*

adapter адаптер *aDAPtir*

address адрес *Adris*

adhesive tape пластырь (*m*) *plaSTYR'*

administrator администратор *adminiSTRAtar*

advance: in advance заранее *zaRAniye*

Africa Африка *Afrika*

after после *POslye*

afternoon: in the afternoon днём *DNYOM;* **good afternoon.** Добрый день. *DObry DYEN'*

ago назад *naZAT*

ahead: straight ahead прямо *PRYAma*

aid помощь (*f*) *POmash*

air mattress надувной матрац *naduvNOY maTRATS*

aircraft самолёт *samaLYOT*

airmail letter авиаписьмо *aviapiS'MO*

airport аэропорт *aeraPORT*

aisle проход *praKHOT*

alarm clock будильник *buDIL'nik*

alcohol спирт *SPIRT*

all (everything) всё *FSYO*

all (everyone) все *FSYE*

allergy аллергия *alirGIya*

allow (may I) разрешить (*p*) *razriSHYT'*

almonds миндаль (*m*) *minDAL'*

almost чуть *CHUT'*

alone (*m*) один *aDIN*

alone (*f*) одна *aDNA*

already уже *uZHE*

also также *TAKzhe*

amalgam амальгама *amal'GAma*

amber янтарь (*m*) *yanTAR'*

ambulance скорая помощь *SKOraya POmash*

America Америка *aMYErika*

American (*m*) американец *amiriKAnits*

American (*f*) американка *amiriKANka*

American американский *amiriKANski*

amethyst аметист *amiTIST*

among среди *sriDI*

amount сумма *SUma*

and и / а *I / A*

ankle лодышка *laDYSHka*

anniversary годовщина *gadafSHIna*

another (more) ещё *yiSHO*

antacid щёлочь (*f*) *SHOlach*

antique store комиссионный магазин *kamisiOny magaZIN*

antiseptic антисептик *antiSYEPtik*

anyone кто-нибудь *KTO-nibut'*

appetizer закуска *zaKUSka*

apple яблоко *YAblaka*

make an appointment (sign up) записаться (*p*) *zapiSAtsa*

appraise оценивать (*i*) *aTSEnivat'*

approach подойти (*p*) *padayTI*

apricot абрикос *abriKOS*

April апрель (*m*) *aPRYEL'*

aquamarine аквамарин *akvamaRIN*

area code код города *KOT GOrada*

arm рука *ruKA*

around вокруг *vaKRUK*

arrive прибывать (*i*) *pribyVAT'*

art искусство *isKUSTva*

artist художник *khuDOZHnik*

ASA ГОСТ *GOST*

ashtray пепельница *PYEpil'nitsa*

ask спрашивать (*i*) *SPRAshivat'*

asparagus спаржа *SPARzha*

aspirin аспирин *aspiRIN*

assortment ассорти (*n*) *asarTI*

at у *U*

attack приступ *PRIstup*

attraction достопримечательность (*f*) *dastaprimiCHAtil'nast'*

auburn каштановый *kaSHTAnavy*

August август *AVgust*

Australia Австралия *afSTRAliya*

Australian (*m*) австралиец *afstraLIyets*

Australian (*f*) австралийка *afstraLIYka*

author автор *AFtar*

authorized авторизованный *aftariZOvany*

automatic автоматический *aftamaTIchiski*

awful ужасно *uZHASna*

B

back спина *spiNA*

back (in the back) сзади *ZAdi*

backwards назад *naZAT*

bad плохой *plaKHOY*

baggage багаж *baGASH;*
  check baggage сдать в
  багаж *ZDAT' v baGASH*

baggage claim check багажная
  бирка *baGAZHnaya BIRka*

baked печёный *piCHOny*

bakery булочная *BUlachnaya*

balcony балкон *balKON*

ball мяч *MYACH*

ballet балет *baLYET*

banana банан *baNAN*

bandage бинт *BINT*

bangs чёлка *CHOLka*

bank банк *BANK*

bar бар *BAR*

bar (of soap, etc.) кусок
  kuSOK

barber shop парикмахерская
  parikMAkhirskaya

bathhouse баня *BAnya*

bathing suit купальник
  kuPAL'nik

bathing trunks плавки
  PLAFki

bathroom туалет *tuaLYET*

battery батарея *bataRYEya*

battery (car) аккумулятор
  akumuLYAtar

be быть (*i*) *BYT'*

beach пляж *PLYASH*

beads бусы *BUsy*

beans фасоль (*f*) *faSOL'*

beard борода *baraDA*

beautiful красивый *kraSIvy*

beauty parlor женский
  салон *ZHENski saLON*

beef Stroganoff беф-строганов
  bif-STROganaf

beer пиво *PIva*

beets свёкла *SVYOkla*

beet soup борщ *BORSH*

before до / перед *DO / PYErit*

begin начинать(ся) (*i*)
  nachiNAtsa

beginning (starting time)
  начало *naCHAla*

behind за *ZA*

bellboy швейцар *shviyTSAR*

belt пояс *POyas*, ремень
  (*m*) *riMYEN'*

Beriozka shop Берёзка
  biRYOSka

better лучше *LUche*

between между *MYEZHdu*

beverage напиток *naPItak*

big большой *bal'SHOY*

bill (check) чек *CHEK*

bill (paper currency) купюра
  kuPYUra

billion миллиард *miliART*

bindings крепления
  kriPLYEniya

bird птица *PTItsa*

birthday день рождения
  DYEN' razhDYEniya; **Happy
  Birthday!** С днём
  рождения! *z DNYOM
  razhDYEniya*

bishop (chess) слон *SLON*

black чёрный *CHORny*

blank form бланк *BLANK*

blanket одеяло *adiYAla*

bleeding кровотечение
  kravatiCHEniye

blender сокавыжиматель
  (*m*) *sakavyzhiMAtil'*

blond белокурый *bilaKUry*

blood кровь (*f*) *KROF'*

blouse блузка *BLUSka*

blow дуть (*i*) *DUT'*

blown glass художественное
  стекло *khuDOzhistvinaye stiKLO*

blue: dark blue синий *SIni;*
  light blue голубой *galuBOY*

board доска *daSKA*

boarding pass посадочный
  талон *paSAdachny taLON*

boat лодка *LOTka,*
  теплоход *tiplaKHOT*

bobby pin шпилка *SHPILka*
body тело *TYEla*
boiled варёный *vaRYOny*
boiling water кипяток *kipiTOK*
Bolshoi Theater Большой театр *bal'SHOY tiATR*
bolt (fastener) болт *BOLT*
Bon voyage! Счастливого пути! *shastLIvava puTI*
bone кость (*f*) *KOST'*
book книга *KNIga*
bookstore книжный магазин *KNIZHny magaZIN*
booth кабина *kaBIna*
boot сапог *saPOK*
bottle бутылка *buTYLka*
bottom дно *DNO*
bouillon бульон *buL'YON*
box ящик *YAshik,* коробка *kaROPka*
box (packet) пакет *paKYET*
box (loge) ложа *LOzha*
bra бюстгальтер *byustGAL'tir*
bracelet браслет *braSLYET*
brake тормоз *TORmas*
brand марка *MARka*
bread хлеб *KHLYEP*
break (recess) перерыв *piriRYF*
break сломать (*p*) *slaMAT'*
breakfast завтрак *ZAFtrak*
breast грудь (*f*) *GRUT'*
breathe дышать (*i*) *dySHAT'*
bridge мост *MOST*
briefcase портфель (*m*) *partFYEL'*
bring принести (*p*) *priniSTI*
British (*m*) англичанин *angliCHAnin*
British (*f*) англичанка *angliCHANka*
British (English) английский *anGLIYski*
broken bone перелом *piriLOM*

brooch брошь (*f*) *BROSH*
brook ручей *ruCHEY*
brother брат *BRAT*
brown коричневый *kaRICHnivy*
bruise ушиб *uSHYP*
brunette брюнетка *bryuNYETka*
brush щётка *SHOTka*
buffet, snack bar буфет *buFYET*
builder строитель (*m*) *straITil'*
building здание *ZDAniye*
bulb лампочка *LAMpachka*
bumper бампер *BAMpir*
bun (hairdo) пучок *puCHOK*
bunch of twigs веник *VYEnik*
bureau (office) бюро *byuRO*
burn ожог *aZHOK*
burn oneself обвариться (*p*) *obvaRItsa*
bus автобус *aFTObus*
business бизнес *BIZnis*
businessman бизнесмен *biznisMYEN*
but а / но *A / NO*
butane gas газ *GAS*
butcher shop магазин "Мясо" *magaZIN MYAsa*
butter масло *MAsla*
button пуговица *PUgavitsa*
buy купить (*p*) *kuPIT*

C

cabbage капуста *kaPUSta*
cabbage soup щи *SHI*
cabin каюта *kaYUta*
cafe кафе *kaFYEY*
cafeteria столовая *staLOvaya*
cake торт *TORT*
call (summon) позвать (*p*) *paZVAT'*

call (telephone) позвонить
(p) *pazvaNIT'*

camera фотоаппарат
fotaapaRAT

can банка *BANka*

can мочь (i) *MOCH*

I can	я могу	*YA maGU*
you can	ты можешь	*TY MOzhish*
he/she can	он/она может	*ON/aNA MOzhit*
we can	мы можем	*MY MOzhim*
you can	вы можете	*VY MOzhitye*
they can	они могут	*aNI MOgut*

Canada Канада *kaNAda*

Canadian (m) канадец
kaNAdits

Canadian (f) канадка
kaNATka

Canadian канадский
kaNATski

candy конфета *kanFYEta*

cap шапочка *SHApachka*

car автомобиль (m)
aftamaBIL', машина
maSHYna

carat карат *kaRAT*

carburetor карбюратор
karbyuRAtar

card карта *KARta*

carefully осторожно
astaROZHna

carp карп *KARP*

carrots морковь (f) *marKOF'*

carry понести (p) *paniSTI*

cart тележка *tiLYEZHka*

carved object резьба *riz'BA*

cash наличные (деньги)
naLICHniye (DYEN'gi)

cashier касса *KAsa*

cassette кассета *kaSYEta*

cassette recorder
магнитофон *magnitaFON*

cathedral собор *saBOR*

Catholic католический
kataLIchiski

cauliflower цветная капуста
tsvitNAya kaPUSta

caution! опасность! (f)
aPASnast'

caviar икра *iKRA;* **black
caviar** зернистая икра
zirNIStaya iKRA; **red caviar**
кетовая икра *KYEtavaya
iKRA*

CD (compact disc)
компактный диск
kamPAKTny DISK

cemetery кладбище
KLADbishe

center середина *siriDIna*

centimeter сантиметр
santiMYETR

central центральный
tsinTRAL'ny

century век *VYEK*

ceramics керамика *kiRAmika*

cereal (cold) крупа *kruPA*

cereal (warm) каша *KAsha*

certified letter ценное письмо
TSEnaye piS'MO

chain цепочка *tsiPOCHka*

chaise longue шезлонг
shizLONG

champagne шампанское
shamPANskaye

change размен *razMYEN*

change разменять (i)
razmiNYAT'

changing room примерочная
кабина *priMYErachnaya
kaBIna*

charge the battery зарядить
аккумулятор *zariDIT'
akumuLYAtar*

charm (jewelry) брелок
briLOK

chassis шасси (n) *shaSI*

cheap, inexpensive дешёвый
diSHOvy

cheaper, less expensive
подешевле *padiSHEvlye*

check (bill) чек *CHEK*

check проверить (p)
praVYErit'

Check! Шах! *SHAKH*

checked в шашечку *f SHAshichku*

checkers шашки *SHASHki*

check-in регистрация *rigiSTRAtsiya*

Checkmate! Мат! *MAT*

check-out time расчётный час *rasSHOTny CHAS*

checkroom камера хранения *KAmira khraNYEniya*

cheek щека *shiKA*

Cheers! На здоровье! *na zdaROv'ye*

cheese сыр *SYR*

cherry вишня *VISHnya*

chess шахматы *SHAKHmaty*

chest cold бронхит *branKHIT*

chestnut каштан *kaSHTAN*

chew жевать (*i*) *zhiVAT'*

chewing tobacco махорка *maKHORka*

chicken курица *KUritsa*, цыплёнок *tsyPLYOnak*

chiffon шифон *shiFON*

children дети *DYEti*

chills озноб *aZNOP*

chocolate шоколадный *shakaLADny*

chop/cutlet отбивная котлета *atbivNAya katLYEta*

church церковь (*f*) *TSERkaf'*

cigarette сигарета *sigaRYEta*

cigar сигар *siGAR*

circle кольцо *kal'TSO*

circle (theater) ярус *YArus*

circus цирк *TSYRK*

citizen (*m*) гражданин *grazhdaNIN*

citizen (*f*) гражданка *grazhDANka*

city город *GOrat*

city tour экскурсия по городу *ekSKURsiya pa GOradu*

class класс *KLAS;* **economy class** туристический класс *turiSTIchiski KLAS*

classical классический *klaSIchiski*

clean почистить (*p*) *paCHIStit'*

cleaned убран *Ubran*

cleansing cream крем для очистки кожи *KRYEM dlya aCHISTki KOzhi*

clinic поликлиника *paliKLInika*

clock часы *chiSY*

close закрывать(ся) (*i*) *zakryVatsa,* закрыть(ся) (*p*) *zaKRYtsa*

closed закрыто *zaKRYta*

clothing одежда *aDYEZHda*

clubs (cards) трефы *TRYEfy*

clutch pedal сцепление *tsiPLYEniye*

coat пальто *pal'TO*

coatroom гардероб *gardiROP*

cod треска *triSKA*

coffee кофе (*m*) *KOfye*

cognac коньяк *kaN'YAK*

cold (in the head) насморк *NASmark*

cold холодный *khaLODny*

colleague коллега *kaLYEga*

collect (telegram) доплатно *daPLATna*

collection сборник *ZBORnik*

collector's stamps коллекционные марки *kaliktsiOniye MARki*

cologne одеколон *adikaLON*

color цвет *TSVYET*

color(ed) цветной *tsvitNOY*

color rinse окраска *aKRASka*

comb расчёска *rasCHOSka*

comb зачёсывать (*i*) *zaCHOsyvat'*

come прийти (*p*) *priyTI*

comedy комедия *kaMYEdiya*

committee комитет *kamiTYET*

communist коммунистический *kamuniSTIchiski*

company фирма *FIRma*

compartment купе *kuPYE*

competition конкуренция *kankuRYENtsiya*

completely совсем *saFSYEM*

computer (adj) компьютерный *kamP'YUtirny*

comrade товарищ *taVArish*

concert концерт *kanTSERT*

conductor (musical) дирижёр *diriZHOR*

confirm потвердить (*p*) *patvirDIT'*

constipation запор *zaPOR*

contact lens контактная линза *kanTAKTnaya LINza*

contract контракт *kanTRAKT*

control контроль (*m*) *kanTROL'*

conversation разговор *razgaVOR*

cookie печенье *piCHEn'ye*

cool прохладный *praKHLADny*

cooperative кооператив *kaapiraTIF*

cooperative кооперативный *kaapiraTIVny*

cop милиционер *militsiaNYER*

cord шнур *SHNUR*

corduroy рубчатый вельвет *RUPchaty vil'VYET*

correct право *PRAva*

correspondent корреспондент *karispanDYENT*

cosmonaut космонавт *kasmaNAFT*

cosmos космос *KOSmas*

cost стоить (*i*) *STOit'*

cot раскладушка *rasklaDUSHka*

cotton вата *VAta*

cotton fabric хлопчатобумажная ткань *khlapchatabuMAZHnaya TKAN'*

cough кашель (*m*) *KAshil'*

cough покашлять (*p*) *paKASHlit'*

cough drops таблетки от кашля *taBLYETki at KASHlya*

cough syrup микстура от кашля *mikSTUra at KASHlya*

count посчитать (*p*) *pashiTAT'*

country страна *straNA*

countryside деревня *diRYEVnya*

coupon, ticket талон *taLON*

course (currency exchange rate) курс *KURS*

cover charge входный билет *FKHODny biLYET*

crab краб *KRAP*

cramp судорога *SUdaraga*

crazy: are you crazy? вы с ума сошли? *VY s uMA saSHLI*

cream сливки *SLIFki*; **whipped cream** взбитые сливки *VZBItiye SLIFki*

cream cheese творог *tvaROK*

credit card кредитная карточка *kriDITnaya KARtachka*

cross country skis беговые лыжи *bigaVIye LYzhi*

crossing (pedestrian) переход *piriKHOT*

crossing (vehicular) переезд *piriYEST*

crown (dental) коронка *kaRONka*

crystal хрусталь (*m*) *khruSTAL'*

cucumber огурец *aguRYETS*

cuisine кухня *KUKHnya*

cupcake кекс *KYEKS*

curls кудри *KUdri*

currants смородина *smaROdina*

currency (foreign—freely convertible) валюта *vaLYUta*

currency exchange point обменный пункт *abMYEny PUNKT*

curve поворот *pavaROT*

customs declaration декларация *diklaRAtsiya*

cut порез *paRYES*

cut oneself порезаться (*p*) *paRYEzatsa*

cuticle scissors маникюрные ножницы *maniKYURniye NOZHnitsy*

cutlet котлета *katLYEta*

D

dacha (country home) дача *DAcha*

dance танцевать (*i*) *tantsiVAT'*

dangerous опасный *aPASny*

dark (*adj*) тёмный *TYOMny*

dark (*adv*) темно *timNO*

darker потемнее *patimNYEye*

darn it! чёрт возьми! *CHORT vaz'MI*

date (calendar) число *chiSLO*

date (fruit) финик *FInik*

daughter дочка *DOCHka*, дочь (*f*) *DOCH*

day день (*m*) *DYEN'*

dead end тупик *tuPIK*

deal (cards) сдавать (*i*) *zdaVAT'*

December декабрь (*m*) *diKABR'*

deck of cards колода *kaLOda*

declaration декларация *diklaRAtsiya*

declare декларировать (*i*) *diklaRIravat'*

deeply глубоко *glubaKO*

degree (of temperature) градус *GRАdus*

delivery доставка *daSTAFka*, поставка *paSTAFka*

deluxe люкс *LYUKS*

dental зубной *zubNOY*

dentist зубной врач *zubNOY VRACH*

denture зубной протез *zubNOY praTYES*

deodorant дезодорант *dizadaRANT*

depart отправляться (*i*) *atpraVLYAtsa*, уезжать (*i*) *uyiZHAT'*

department store универмаг *univirMAK*

deposit (security) залог *zaLOK*

deposit slip приходный ордер *priKHODny ORdir*; **make a deposit** выдать вклад *VYdat' FKLAT*

desk стол *STOL*

dessert сладкое *SLATkaye*

detour объезд *aBYEST*

develop (film) проявлять (*i*) *prayiVLYAT'*

devil чёрт *CHORT*

dial набирать (*i*) *nabiRAT'*

diamond бриллиант *briliANT*

diamonds (cards) бубны *BUBny*

diaper пелёнка *piLYONka*

diarrhea понос *paNOS*

dictionary словарь (*m*) *slaVAR'*

digital watch электронные часы *elikTROniye chiSY*

dinner ужин *Uzhin*

diplomat дипломат *diplaMAT*

direction направление *napravLYEniye*

directional signal сигнальный огонь *sigNAL'ny aGON'*

disconnect разъединить *(p) razyidiNIT'*

discotheque дискотека *diskaTYEka*

disc, disk диск *DISK*

dish блюдо *BLYUda*

dislocated вывихнут *VYvykhnut*

disposable diapers бумажная пелёнка *buMAZHnaya piLYONka*

dizzy:I'm dizzy голова кружится *galaVA KRUzhitsa*

do сделать *(p) ZDYElat'*

dock пристань *(f) PRIstan'*

doctor врач *VRACH*

dollar доллар *DOlar*

door дверь *(f) DVYER'*

down вниз *VNIS*

downhill skis горные лыжи *GORniye LYzhi*

downtown центр *TSENTR*

drama (tragedy) трагедия *traGYEdiya*

dress платье *PLAt'ye*

dress (oneself) одеваться *(i) adiVAtsa*

drink пить *(i) PIT'*, выпить *(p) VYpit'*

drive by заехать *(p) zaYEkhat'*

driver водитель *(m) vaDItil'*

driver's license водительские права *vaDItil'skiye praVA*

drop капля *KAplya*

drop уронить *(p) uraNIT'*

drugstore аптека *apTYEka*

dry сухой *suKHOY*

dry cleaner's химчистка *khimCHISTka*

dry cleaning чистка *CHISTka*

duck утка *UTka*

during во время *va VRYEmya*

duty (customs) пошлина *POSHlina*

E

each каждый *KAZHdy*

ear ухо *Ukha*

ear drops ушные капли *ushNIye KApli*

early рано *RAna*

earring серьга *sir'GA*

east восток *vaSTOK*

easy лёгкий *LYOki*

edition издание *iZDAniye*

egg яйцо *yayTSO;* **hard-boiled egg** яйцо вкрутую *yayTSO fkruTUyu;* **soft-boiled egg** яйцо всмятку *yayTSO FSMYATku*

eggplant баклажан *baklaZHAN*

eight восемь *VOsim'*

eight hundred восемьсот *vasim'SOT*

eighteen восемнадцать *vasimNAtsat'*

eighth восьмой *vaS'MOY*

eighty восемьдесят *VOsim'disit*

elbow локоть *(m) LOkat'*

elderly пожилой *pazhiLOY*

electrical электрический *elikTRIchiski*

elevator лифт *LIFT*

eleven одиннадцать *aDInatsat'*

embassy посольство *paSOL'stva*

emerald изумруд *izumRUT*

emergency exit запасный выход *zaPASny VYkhat*

end конец *kaNETS*

end кончать(ся) *(i) kanCHAtsa*

engagement/wedding ring обручальное кольцо *abruCHAL'naye kal'TSO*

England Англия *ANgliya*

English английский *anGLIYski*

enlarge увеличить *(p) uviLIchit'*

enough хватить *(p) KHVAtit'*

enter, come in входить *(i) fkhaDIT'*

enterprise предприятие *pridpriYAtiye*

entirely совсем *saFSYEM*

entrance вход *FKHOT*

entrance ticket, cover charge входной билет *fkhadNOY biLYET*

entry въезд *VYEST*

envelope конверт *kanVYERT*

eraser ластик *LAStik*

err ошибиться *(p) ashiBItsa*

escort проводить *(i) pravaDIT'*

etc., et cetera и т. д., и так далее *I TAK DAliye*

even out подравнять *(p) padravNYAT'*

evening вечер *VYEchir;* **in the evening** вечером *VYEchiram;* **good evening!** добрый вечер! *DObry VYEchir*

everyone все *FSYE*

everything всё *FSYO*

except кроме *KROmye*

exchange обменять *(i) abmiNYAT'*

exchange rate обменный курс *abMYEny KURS*

excursion экскурсия *ekSKURsiya*

excuse извинить *(p) izviNIT';* **excuse me!** извините! *izviNItye*

exhaust pipe выхлопная трубка *vykhlapNAya TRUPka*

exhibition выставка *VYstafka*

exit выход *VYkhat*

exit выходить *(i) vykhaDIT'*, выйти *(p) VYti*

expenses затраты *zaTRAty,* расходы *rasKHOdy*

expensive дорогой *daraGOY;* **more expensive** подороже *padaROzhe*

exposure кадр *KADR*

extension cord удлинитель *(m) udliNItil'*

extra лишний *LISHni*

extra (spare) запасный *zaPASny*

eye глаз *GLAS*

eye drops глазные капли *glazNIye KApli*

eyebrow бровь *(f) BROF'*

F

fabric ткань *(f) TKAN'*

face лицо *liTSO*

fall осень *(f) Osin';* **in the fall** осенью *Osin'yu*

fall упасть *(p) uPAST'*

false tooth вставной зуб *fstavNOY ZUP*

family семья *siM'YA*

family name фамилия *faMIliya*

fan вентилятор *vintiLYAtar*

fan belt ремень вентилятора *riMYEN' vintiLYAtara*

far далеко *daliKO*

farewell! прощайте! *praSHAYtye*

fast быстрый *BYStry*

father отец *aTYETS*

faucet смеситель *(m) smiSItil'*

fax телефакс *tiliFAKS*

February февраль (*m*) *fiVRAL'*

fee плата *PLAta*

feed кормить (*i*) *karMIT'*

feel чувствовать себя (*i*) *CHUSTvavat' siBYA*

felt войлок *VOYlak*

fender решётка *riSHOTka*

fever жар *ZHAR*; **I have a fever** у меня температура *u miNYA timpiraTUra*

few несколько *NYEskal'ka*

field поле *POlye*

fifteen пятнадцать *pitNAtsat'*

fifth пятый *PYAty*

fifty пятьдесят *pidiSYAT*

fig фига *FIga*

figure skates фигурные коньки *fiGURniye kan'KI*

filet of sturgeon балык *baLYK*

filling (dental) пломба *PLOMba*

film (photographic) плёнка *PLYONka*

filter фильтр *FIL'TR*

find найти (*p*) *nayTI*

finger палец *PAlits*

fingernail ноготь (*m*) *NOgat'*

fire пожар *paZHAR*

first первый *PYERvy*

fish рыба *RYba*

five пять *PYAT'*

five hundred пятьсот *pit'SOT*

fix чинить (*i*) *chiNIT'*, починить (*p*) *pachiNIT'*

flannel фланель (*f*) *flaNYEL'*

flash вспышка *FSPYSHka*

flashlight фонарь (*m*) *faNAR'*

flight полёт *paLYOT*

flints кремни *krimNI*

floor этаж *eTASH*

flowers цветы *tsviTY*

folk народ *naROT*

folk music народная музыка *naRODnaya MUzyka*

food блюдо *BLYUda*

fool дурак *duRAK*

foot ступня *stupNYA*

for для *DLYA*

foreign иностранный *inaSTRAny*

forest лес *LYES*

fork вилка *VILka*

forty сорок *SOrak*

four четыре *chiTYrye*

four hundred четыреста *chiTYrista*

foursome четверо *CHETvira*

fourteen четырнадцать *chiTYRnatsat'*

fourth четвёртый *chitVYORty*

fox лиса *liSA*

frame (for glasses) оправа *aPRAva*

free (vacant) свободный *svaBODny*

fresh свежий *SVYEzhi*

Friday пятница *PYATnitsa*

fried жареный *ZHAriny*

friend друг *DRUK*

from из *IS*, от *OT*, с *S*

front (in front) перед *PYErit*, спереди *SPYEridi*

fruits фрукты *FRUKty*

fuel pump бензонасос *binzanaSOS*

fund фонд *FONT*

fur мех *MYEKH*

fur меховой *mikhaVOY*

future будущий *BUdushi*

G

gabardine габардин *gabarDIN*

gallery галерея *galiRYEya*

gallon галлон *gaLON*

garden сад *SAT*

garlic чеснок *chiSNOK*

gas (butane) газ *GAS*

gasoline бензин *binZIN*

gas tank бензобак *binzaBAK*

gauze (sanitary) napkin марлевая салфетка *MARlivaya salFYETka*

gear скорость (*f*) *SKOrast'*

gear shift сцепление *tsiPLYEniye*

general delivery до востребования *da vasTRYEbavaniya*

get off выйти (*p*) *VYti*

get to проехать (*p*) *praYEkhat'*

gift подарок *paDArak*

give дать (*p*) *DAT'*

glass стакан *staKAN*

glasses очки *achKI*

gloss гланц *GLANTS*

glove перчатка *pirCHATka*

glue клей *KLYEY*

go by foot идти (*i*) *iTI*

go by vehicle ехать (*i*) *YEkhat'*

gold золото *ZOlata*

gold(en) золотой *zalaTOY*

gold-plated позолоченый *pazaLOchiny*

good хороший *khaROshi*

good-bye! до свидания! *da sviDAniya*

goodness: my goodness! боже мой! *BOzhe MOY*

goods, items товары *taVAry*

goose гусь (*m*) *GUS'*

gram грамм *GRAM*

grape виноград *vinaGRAT*

grapefruit грейпфрут *GRYEYPfrut*

gray серый *SYEry*

grease смазать (*p*) *SMAzat'*

great великий *viLIki*

Grill Гриль (*m*) *GRIL'*

grilled обжаренный *abZHAriny*

group группа *GRUpa*

guidebook путеводитель (*m*) *putivaDItil'*

GUM ГУМ *GUM*

gum десна *diSNA*

H

hair волос *vaLOS*

haircut стрижка *STRISHka;* **have a haircut** постричься (*p*) *paSTRICHtsa*

hairdo причёска *priCHOSka*

hair dryer фен *FYEN*

hair spray лак для волос *LAK dlya vaLOS*

half половина *palaVIna*

hall зал *ZAL*

ham ветчина *vichiNA*

hammer молоток *malaTOK*

hand кисть (*f*) *KIST'*

hand brake ручной тормоз *ruchNOY TORmas*

handicapped инвалид *invaLIT*

handkerchief носовой платок *nasaVOY plaTOK*

handle ручка *RUCHka*

hanger вешалка *VYEshalka*

happen случиться (*p*) *sluCHItsa*

hat шапка *SHAPka*

have/there is есть *YEST'*

hay fever сенная лихорадка *SYEnaya likhaRATka*

he он *ON*

head голова *galaVA*

headache головная боль *galavNAya BOL'*

headlight фара *FAra*

health здоровье *zdaROv'ye*

heart сердце *SYERtse*

heart attack сердечный приступ *sirDYECHny PRIstup*

hearts (cards) черви *CHERvi*

hectare гектар *gikTAR*

heel каблук *kaBLUK*

height рост *ROST*

hello! здравствуйте! *ZDRASTvuytye*

help помочь *(p) paMOCH*

here здесь *ZDYES'*

here it is вот оно *VOT aNO*

herring селёдка *siLYOTka*

herringbone ёлочка *YOlachka*

high высокий *vySOki*

hill холм *KHOLM*

hip бедро *biDRO*

history история *iSTOriya*

hockey хоккей *khaKYEY*

hockey skates хоккейные коньки *khaKYEYniye kan'KI*

holiday праздник *PRAZnik*

home / house дом *DOM*

at home дома *DOma*

(to) home домой *daMOY*

hood капот *kaPOT*

horn гудок *guDOK*

hospital больница *bal'NItsa*

hospitality гостеприимство *gastipriIMstva*

hot (temperature) жаркий *ZHARki*

hot (object) горячий *gaRYAchi*

hotel гостиница *gaSTInitsa*

hour час *CHAS*

household хозяйственный *khaZYAYSTviny*

how как *KAK*

how many, how much сколько *SKOL'ka*

humor юмор *YUmar*

hundred сто *STO*

hungry *(m)* голоден *GOladin*

hungry *(f)* голодна *galaDNA*

hurry спешить *(i) spiSHYT'*

hurt болеть *(i) baLYET'*; **it hurts** болит *baLIT*; **that hurts** больно *BOL'na*

husband муж *MUSH*

I

I я *YA*

ice лёд *LYOT*

ice skates коньки *kan'KI*

if если *YEsli*

ignition зажигание *zazhiGAniye*

in в *V*

inch дюйм *DYUYM*

(be) included входить *(i) fkhaDIT'*

inexpensive дешёвый *diSHOvy*

infection инфекция *inFYEKtsiya*

information информация *infarMAtsiya*

initial первоначальный *pirvanaCHAL'ny*

inside внутри *vnuTRI*

insole стелька *STYEL'ka*

insomnia бессонница *biSOnitsa*

inspection инспекция *inSPYEKtsiya*

institute институт *instiTUT*

instrument инструмент *instruMYENT*

insurance страхование *strakhaVAniye*

intermission антракт *anTRAKT*

international международный *mizhdunaRODny*

interpreter переводчик *piriVOTchik*

into в *V*

Intourist Интурист *intuRIST*

introduce (oneself) представить(ся) *(p) pritSTAvit'/pritSTAvitsa*

invite пригласить *(p) priglaSIT'*

iodine йод *YOT*

ironing глажка *GLASHka*

item штука *SHTUka*

ivory слоновая кость *slaNOvaya KOST'*

J

jack (car) домкрат *damKRAT*

jack (cards) валет *vaLYET*

jacket пиджак *pidZHAK*

jade нефрит *niFRIT*

January январь (m) *yinVAR'*

jasper яшма *YASHma*

jeans джинсы *DZHYNsy*

jelly варенье *vaRYEn'ye*

jewelry store ювелирный магазин *yuviLIRny magaZIN*

juice сок *SOK*

julienne жульен *zhuL'YEN*

July июль (m) *iYUL'*

June июнь (m) *iYUN'*

junior младший *MLADshi*

just in case (string bag) авоська *aVOS'ka*

K

key ключ *KLYUCH*

key card (pass) пропуск *PROpusk*

"key lady" дежурная *diZHURnaya*

kidney soup рассольник *raSOL'nik*

kilo(gram) кило (грамм) *kiLO / kilaGRAM*

kilometer километр *kilaMYETR*

king король (m) *kaROL'*

kiosk киоск *kiOSK*

knee колено *kaLYEna*

knife нож *NOSH*

knight (chess) офицер *afiTSER*

knock over сбить (p) *ZBIT'*

know знать (i) *ZNAT'*

know how уметь (i) *uMYET'*

kopeck копейка *kaPYEYka*

Kremlin Кремль (m) *KRYEML'*

L

lace кружева *kruzhiVA*

ladies' женский *ZHENski*

lake озеро *Ozira*

lamb баранина *baRAnina*

lamp лампа *LAMpa*

land приплывать (i) *priplyVAT'*

language язык *yiZYK*

lapel pin значок *znaCHOK*

large крупный *KRUPny*

larger больше *BOL'she*

last длиться (i) *DLItsa*

late поздно *POZna*

(be) late опаздывать (i) *aPAZdyvat'*

later позже *POzhe*

laundromat прачечная самообслуживания *PRAchichnaya samaapSLUzhivaniya*

laundry прачечная *PRAchichnaya*

lawyer адвокат *advaKAT*

laxative слабительное *slaBItil'naye*

leak протекать (i) *pratiKAT'*

lean прислоняться (i) *prislaNYAtsa*

leather кожа *KOzha*

leave, depart отправляться (i) *atpraVLYAtsa*

leave (something) оставить (p) *aSTAvit'*

left левый *LYEvy;* **to the left** налево *naLYEva;* **on the left** слева *SLYEva*

leg нога *naGA*

lemon лимон *liMON*

lend одолжить (*p*) *adalZHYT'*

length длинна *dliNA*

Lenin Ленин *LYEnin*

Leningrad Ленинград *lininGRAT*

lens (eyeglass) стекло *stiKLO*

lens (contact) контактная линза *kanTAKTnaya LINza*

less меньше *MYEN'she*

let (allow) пусть *PUST'*

let in пускать (*i*) *puSKAT'*

letter письмо *piS'MO*

lettuce салат *saLAT*

library библиотека *bibliaTYEka*

lie (in bed) лежать (*i*) *liZHAT'*

lie down ложиться (*i*) *laZHYtsa*, лечь (*p*) *LYECH*

lifeguard спасатель (*m*) *spaSAtil'*

light светлый *SVYETly*

lighter зажигалка *zazhiGALka*

like, be pleasing to нравиться *NRAvitsa*

like, love любить (*i*) *lyuBIT'*

I'd like мне хочется *MNYE KHOchitsa*

lined paper бумага в линейку *buMAga v liNYEYku*

linen полотно *palatNO*

linen towel, sheet простыня *praSTYnya*

lip губа *GUba*

lipstick губная помада *gubNAya paMAda*

liqueur ликёр *liKYOR*

list список *SPIsak*

listen слушать (*i*) *SLUshat'*

liter литр *LITR*

little немного *niMNOga*, мало *MAla*

liver печень (*f*) *PYEchin'*

loaf батон *baTON*

long длинный *DLIny*

(a) long time долго *DOLga*

long distance call международный разговор *mizhdugaRODny razgaVOR*

look смотреть (*i*) *smaTRYET'*

look at взглянуть (*p*) *vzgliNUT'*

lose потерять(ся) (*p*) *patiRYAtsa*

lose a game проиграть (*p*) *praiGRAT'*

lotion крем *KRYEM*, лосьон *laS'YON*

loud громко *GROMka*

lousy плохо *PLOkha*

love любить (*i*) *lyuBIT'*

lunch обед *aBYET*

M

magazine журнал *zhurNAL*

magnesia магнезия *magNYEziya*

mail почта *POCHta*

mailbox почтовый ящик *pachTOvy YAshik*

main главный *GLAVny*

maitre d'hotel метрдотель (*m*) *mitradaTYEL'*

make сделать (*p*) *ZDYElat'*

make-up мэйк-ап *meyk-AP*

malachite малахит *malaKHIT*

Maly Theater Малый театр *MAly tiATR*

man мужчина *mushCHIna*; **young man** молодой человек *malaDOY chilaVYEK*

manager заведующий *zaVYEduyushi*

manicure маникюр *maniKYUR*

many, much много *MNOga*; **how many?** сколько? *SKOL'ka*

map план *PLAN*

March март *MART*

market рынок *RYnak*

marmot сурок *suROK*

married: are you married? (of a man) вы женаты? *VY zhiNAty;* **are you married? (of a woman)** вы замужем? *VY ZAmuzhim*

mascara тушь для ресниц *TUSH dlya risNITS*

massage массаж *maSASH*

matches спички *SPICHki*

material, fabric ткань (*f*) *TKAN'*

matte матовый *MAtavy*

matter дело *DYEla*

mattress матрац *maTRATS*

mausoleum мавзолей *mavzaLYEY*

maximum максимальный *maksiMAL'ny*

may (one) можно *MOZHna*

maybe может быть *MOzhit BYT'*

mayonnaise майонез *mayaNYES*

mead медовуха *midaVUkha*

mean значить (*i*) *ZNAchit'*

meat мясо *MYAsa*

medicine лекарство *liKARSTva*

medium средний *SRYEDni*

meeting встреча *FSTRYEcha*

melon дыня *DYnya*

memory память (*f*) *PAmit'*

men's мужской *mushSKOY*

menthol ментол *minTOL*

menu меню *miNYU*

meter метр *MYETR*

Metro метро *miTRO*

mezzanine бельэтаж *bileTASH*

midnight полночь (*f*) *POLnach*

mild слабый *SLAby*

milk молоко *malaKO*

millimeter миллиметр *miliMYETR*

million миллион *miliON*

mind ум *UM*

mine, my мой, моя, мое, мои *MOY, maYA, maYO, maI*

mineral water минеральная вода *miniRAL'naya vaDA*

minimal минимальный *miniMAL'ny*

minister пастор *PAStar*

mink норка *NORka*

minute минута *miNUta;* **just a minute!** минуточку! *miNUtachku*

mirror зеркало *ZYERkala*

Miss, Mrs. госпожа *gaspaZHA*

miss! девушка! *DYEvushka*

Mister господин *gaspaDIN*

mitten рукавица *rukaVItsa*

mixture микстура *mikSTUra*

modern современный *savriMYEny*

monastery монастырь (*m*) *manaSTYR'*

Monday понедельник *paniDYEL'nik*

money деньги *DYEN'gi*

money order денежный перевод *DYEnizhny piriVOT*

month месяц *MYEsits*

monument памятник *PAmitnik*

more больше *BOL'she*

morning утро *Utra;* **in the morning** утром *Utram;* **good morning** доброе утро *DObraye Utra*

Moscow Москва *maskVA*

mosque мечеть (*f*) *miCHET'*

mother мать (*f*) *MAT'*

mountain гора *gaRA*

mouth рот *ROT*

mouthwash зубной эликсир *zubNOY elikSIR*

movie фильм *FIL'M*

much много *MNOga*

muffin кекс *KYEKS*

museum музей *muZYEY*

mushroom гриб *GRIP*

music музыка *MUzyka*

musical музыкальный *muzyKAL'ny*

must надо *NAda*

mustache усы *uSY*

mustard горчица *garCHItsa*

mustard plaster горчичник *garCHICHnik*

myself (*m*) сам *SAM*

myself (*f*) сама *saMA*

mystery (film, novel) детектив *ditikTIF*

N

nail clippers кусачки *kuSACHki*

nail file пилка *PILka*

nail polish remover ацетон *atsiTON*

name: first name имя (*n*) *Imya;* **patronymic** отчество *Ochstva;* **family name** фамилия *faMIliya;* **my name is** меня зовут *miNYA zaVUT;* **what is your name?** как вас зовут? *KAK VAS zaVUT*

napkin салфетка *salFYETka*

narrow (too tight) тесны *tiSNY*

nationality национальность (*f*) *natsiaNAL'nast'*

nausea тошнота *tashnaTA*

near близко *BLISka*

nearby поблизости *paBLIzasti*

nearest ближайший *bliZHAYshi*

necessary нужно *NUZHna*

neck шея *SHEya*

necklace ожерелье *azhiRYEl'ye*

need
I need
мне нужен   *MNYE NUzhin*
мне нужна   *MNYE nuzhNA*
мне нужно   *MNYE NUZHna*
мне нужны   *MNYE nuzhNY*

needle иголка *iGOLka*

nested doll матрёшка *maTRYOSHka*

never никогда *nikagDA*

new новый *NOvy*

newspaper газета *gaZYEta*

newsstand газетный киоск *gaZYETny kiOSK*

next следующий *SLYEduyushi*

night ночь (*f*) *NOCH;* **good night!** спокойной ночи! *spaKOYnay NOchi*

nightclub ночной бар *nachNOY BAR*

nine девять *DYEvit'*

nine hundred девятьсот *divit'SOT*

nineteen девятнадцать *divitNAtsat'*

ninety девяносто *diviNOSta*

ninth девятый *diVYAty*

no нет *NYET*

nonprescription безрецептный *bizriTSEPTny*

non-smoking некуряший *nikuRYAshi*

nonsense ерунда *yirunDA*

noodles лапша *lapSHA*

noodle soup суп-лапша *SUP-lapSHA*

noon полдень (*m*) *POLdin'*

no one никто *niKTO*

normal нормальный *narMAL'ny*

north север *SYEvir*

nose нос *NOS*

not не *NYE*

notebook тетрадь (*f*) *tiTRAT'*

nothing ничего *nichiVO*

novel роман *raMAN*

November ноябрь (*m*) *naYABR'*

now сейчас *siCHAS*

number номер *NOmir*, число *chiSLO*

nurse медсестра *midsiSTRA*

nut гайка *GAYka*

nut (food) орех *aRYEKH*

nylon нейлон *niyLON*

O

oatmeal овсянный *aFSYAny*

obligation обязательство *abiZAtil'stva*

occupied занято *ZAnita*

o'clock (hour) час *CHAS*

October октябрь (*m*) *akTYABR'*

of course конечно *kaNYESHna*

office канцелярский *kantsiLYARski*

often часто *CHASta*

oil масло *MAsla*

ointment мазь (*f*) *MAS'*

on на *NA*

once раз *RAS*

oncoming встречный *FSTRYECHny*

one (*m*) один *aDIN*

one (*f*) одна *aDNA*

oneself себе, себя *siBYE, siBYA*

onion лук *LUK*

only только *TOL'ka*

on time вовремя *VOvrimya*

onto на *NA*

onyx оникс *Oniks*

open открывать(ся) (*i*) *atkryVAtsa*, открыть(ся) (*p*) *atKRYtsa*

opened открыто *atKRYta*

opera опера *Opira*

opera glasses бинокль (*m*) *biNOKL'*

operetta оперетта *apiRYEta*

opposite напротив *naPROtif*

optician оптика *OPtika*

or или *Ili*

orange (*n*) апельсин *apil'SIN*

orange (*adj*) апельсиновый *apil'SInavy*

orchestra seat партер *parTYER*

order порядок *paRYAdak*

order заказывать (*i*) *zaKAzyvat'*, заказать (*p*) *zakaZAT'*

Orthodox православный *pravaSLAVny*

ouch! ой! *OY*

our наш, наша, наше, наши *NASH, NAsha, NAshe, NAshi*

outside вне *VNYE*

overheat перегреваться (*i*) *pirigriVAtsa*

owe
I owe (*m*) я должен *YA DOLzhin*
I owe (*f*) я должна *YA dalzhNA*
You owe Вы должны *VY dalzhNY*

P

pack пачка *PACHka*

package посылка *paSYLka*

packet пакет *paKYET*

page страница *straNItsa*

pair пара *PAra*

pajamas пижама *piZHAma*

palace дворец *dvaRYETS*

Palace of Congresses Дворец съездов *dvaRYETS SYEZdaf*

pancake house блинная *BLInaya*

panties трусики *TRUsiki*

pants брюки *BRYUki*

pantyhose колготки *kalGOTki*

paper бумага *buMAga*

paper бумажный *buMAZHny*

paper clip скрепка *SKRYEPka*

pardon простить (*i*) *praSTIT'*

pardon me! простите! *praSTItye*

park парк *PARK*

parking стоянка *staYANka*

part часть (*f*) *CHAST'*

part (in the hair) пробор *praBOR*

partial частичный *chaSTICHny*

partner партнёр *partNYOR*

party (political) партия *PARtiya*

pass by проходить (*i*) *prakhaDIT'*

passenger пассажир *pasaZHYR*

passing обгон *abGON*

passport паспорт *PASpart*

past прошлый *PROshly*

paste паста *PASta*

pastry пирожное *piROZHnaye*

path дорожка *daROSHka*, путь (*m*) *PUT'*, тропинка *traPINka*

patronymic отчество *Ochistva*

pawn (chess) пешка *PYESHka*

pay платить (*i*) *plaTIT'*

pay telephone телефон-афтомат *tilFON aftaMAT*

payment оплата *aPLAta*, плата *PLAta*, платёж *plaTYOSH*

peach персик *PYERsik*

pear груша *GRUsha*

pearl жемчуг *ZHEMchuk*

pedestrian пешеходный *pishiKHODny*

pelmeni (Siberian dumplings) пельмени *pil'MYEni*

pen ручка *RUCHka*

pencil карандаш *karanDASH*

penicillin пеницилин *pinitsiLIN*

people's народный *naRODny*

pepper перец *PYErits*

performance спектакль (*m*) *spikTAKL'*

perfume духи *duKHI*

permanent химическая завивка *khiMIchiskaya zaVIFka*

person to person на человека *na chilaVYEka*

personal личный *LICHny*

pharmacy аптека *apTYEka*

pheasant фасан *faSAN*

phone позвонить (*p*) *pazvaNIT'*

photograph фотографировать (*i*) *fatagraFIravat'*

phrasebook разговорник *razgaVORnik*

pick up (drive by) заехать (*p*) *zaYEkhat'*

picture картина *karTIna*

picture (photo) фотография *fataGRAfiya*

pie пирог *piROK*

piece (chess) фигура *fiGUra*

pike perch судак *suDAK*

pillow подушка *paDUSHka*

pin булавка *buLAFka*

pinch жать (*i*) *ZHAT'*

pineapple ананас *anaNAS*

pink розовый *ROzavy*

pipe трубка *TRUPka*

pipe tobacco трубочный табак *TRUbachny taBAK*

place место *MYESta*

plaid в клетку *f KLYETku*

plans планы *PLAny*

plant растение *raSTYEniye*

plate тарелка *taRYELka*

platform платформа *platFORma*

platinum платина *PLAtina*

play играть (*i*) *iGRAT'*

please пожалуйста *paZHAlusta*

pleasing приятно *priYATna*

pleasure удовольствие *udaVOL'stviye;* **with pleasure** с удовольствием *s udaVOL'stviyim*

pliers плоскогубцы *plaskaGUPtsy*

plug розетка *raZYETka*

plum слива *SLIva*

pocket (*adj*) карманный *karMAny*

pocketbook сумка *SUMka*

poetry стихотворение *stikhatvaRYEniye*

point пункт *PUNKT*

pole палка *PALka*

police милиция *miLItsiya*

polka dot горошек *gaROshik*

polyclinic поликлиника *paliKLInika*

polyester полиэфир *palieFIR*

pomegranate гранат *graNAT*

pond пруд *PRUT*

pony tail хвост *KHVOST*

poplin поплин *paPLIN*

popular популярный *papuLYARny*

porcelain фарфоровый *farFOravy*

pork свиной *sviNOY*

porter носильщик *naSIL'shik*

post office почта *POCHta*

postcard открытка *atKRYTka*

poster плакат *plaKAT*

potatoes картофель (*m*) *karTOfil'*

pound фунт *FUNT*

powder пудра *PUdra*

practically практически *prakTIchiski*

prefer предпочитать (*i*) *pritpachiTAT'*

prescription рецепт *riTSEPT*

press гладить (*i*) *GLAdit'*

price цена *tsiNA*

priest священник *sviSHEnik*

printed matter бандероль (*f*) *bandiROL'*

private taxi частник *CHASnik*

problem проблема *praBLYEma*

process процесс *praTSES*

profession профессия *praFYEsiya*

profit прибыль (*f*) *PRIbyl'*

program программа *praGRAMka*

prohibited запрещено *zaprishiNO*

Protestant протестантский *pratiSTANTski*

pull! (toward oneself) к себе *k siBYE*

pull (a tooth) удалить (*p*) *udaLIT'*

pump насос *naSOS*

pumpkin тыква *TYKva*

punch (a ticket) пробить (*p*) *praBIT'*

purchase покупка *paKUPka*

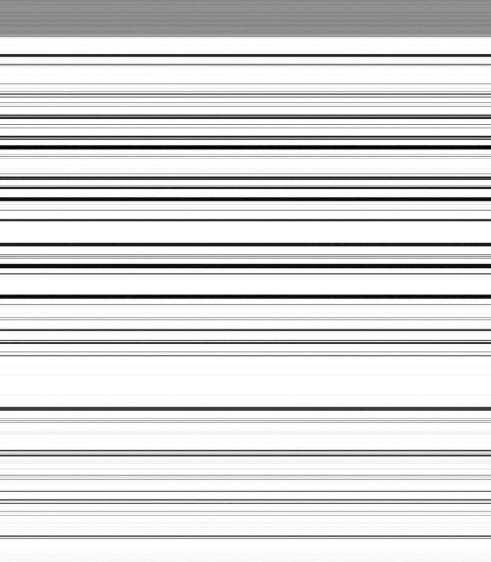

restrictio
agrani

restroom
туале
tuaLY
туале

retail pri
ROZni

return
there a
обрат

return
vazvra
(p) *vi*

revolution
rivaLY

rib ребр

rice рис

ride про

right пра
right
on the
SPRAva

right of wa
priiMUs

ring кол

ring (theat

river рек

road дор

road map
карта
KARta

roast beef

robe хала

roll було

roll (of som
ruLON

rook (chess

room (hotel

rouge ру м

row ряд

rubber ban

ruble руб

ruby руби

ruler лин

science-fiction научно-популярный *naUCHna-papuLYARny*

scissors ножницы *NOZHnitsy*

score счёт *SHOT*

Scotch tape скотч *SKOTCH*

scrambled eggs яичница-болтунья *yaICHnitsa-balTUn'ya*

screw винтик *VINtik*

screwdriver отвёртка *atVYORTka*

sea море *MOrye*

sea sickness морская болезнь *marSKAya baLYEZN'*

seasoning приправа *priPRAva*

seat место *MYESta*

second (sixtieth part of a minute) секунда *siKUNda*

second второй *ftaROY*

section отдел *aDYEL*

security безопасность (f) *bizaPASnast'*

sedative успокаивающее *uspaKAivayushiye*

see смотреть (i) *smaTRYET'*

seem казаться (i) *kaZAtsa*

self сам *SAM*

sell продавать (i) *pradaVAT'*

semi-dry полусухое *palusuKHOye*

send послать (p) *paSLAT'*

senior старший *STARshi*

separately отдельно *aDYEL'na*

September сентябрь (m) *sinTYABR'*

seriously серьёзно *siR'YOZna*

service обслуживание *apSLUzhivaniye*

service bureau бюро обслуживание *byuRO apSLUzhivaniya*

service (religious) служба *SLUZHba*

service station бензоколонка *binzakaLONka*

set (hairdo) укладка *uKLATka*

seven семь *SYEM'*

seven hundred семьсот *sim'SOT*

seventeen семнадцать *simNAtsat'*

seventh седьмой *sid'MOY*

seventy семьдесят *SYEM'disit*

sew пришить (p) *priSHYT'*

shadow тень (f) *TYEN'*

shame: what a shame! как жаль! *KAK ZHAL'*

shampoo шампунь (m) *shamPUN'*

sharpener точилка *taCHILka*

shave побриться (p) *paBRItsa*

she она *aNA*

sheepskin овчина *afCHIna*

shift (gear) сцепление *tsiPLYEniye*

shine светить (i) *SVYEtit'*

shipment отправка *atPRAFka*

shirt рубашка *ruBASHka*, сорочка *saROCHka*

shoelace шнурок *shnuROK*

shoes обувь (f) *Obuf'*; **men's shoes** ботинки *baTINki*; **women's shoes** туфли *TUfli*

shop, store магазин *magaZIN*

short короткий *kaROTki*

shoulder плечо *pliCHO*

show варьете *var'yiTE*

show показать (p) *pakaZAT'*

shower душ *DUSH*

shuffle перетасовать (p) *piriTAsavat'*

shut up (keep silent) молчать (i) *malCHAT'*

sick: I feel sick я заболел *YA zabaLYEL*

sickness болезнь (f) *baLYEZN'*

side сторона *staraNA*

side бок *BOK*

sideburn височка *viSOCHka*

sign расписаться (*p*) *raspiSAtsa*

signal сигнальный *sigNAL'ny*

silk шёлк *SHOLK*

silver (*n*) серебро *siriBRO*

silver (*adj*) серебряный *siRYEbriny*

sing петь (*i*) *PYET'*

single ticket единый билет *yiDIny biLYET*

sink умывальник *umyVAL'nik*

sister сестра *siSTRA*

sit сидеть (*i*) *siDYET'*, посидеть (*p*) *pasiDYET'*

six шесть *SHEST'*

six hundred шестьсот *shist'SOT*

sixteen шестнадцать *shistNAtsat'*

sixth шестой *shiSTOY*

sixty шестьдесят *shizdiSYAT*

size размер *razMYER*

skate кататься на коньках *kaTAtsa na kan'KAKH*

skates коньки *kan'KI*

ski кататься на лыжах *kaTAtsa na LYzhakh*

skin кожа *KOzha*

skirt юбка *YUPka*

skis лыжи *LYzhi*

slacks штаны *shtaNY*

sled санки *SANki*

sleeping pills снотворное *snaTVORnaye*

sleeve рукав *ruKAF*

slide слайд *SLAYT*

slip (ladies') комбинация *kambiNAtsiya*

slipper тапочка *TApachka*

slippery скользкий *SKOL'ski*

slow медленный *MYEdliny*

small мелкий *MYEL'ki*

smaller меньше *MYEN'she*

smile улыбаться (*i*) *ulyBAtsa*

smoke курить (*i*) *kuRIT'* закурить (*p*) *zakuRIT'*

smoking курящий *kuRYAshi*

smorgasbord шведский стол *SHVYETski STOL*

snack bar закусочная *zaKUsachnaya*

snow снег *SNYEK*

so так *TAK*

soap мыло *MYla*

soccer футбол *fudBOL*

socialist социалистический *satsialiSTIchiski*

sock носок *naSOK*

soft мягкий *MYAki*

soft drink лимонад *limaNAT*

sole (shoe) подмётка *padMYOTka*

solid-color однотонное *adnaTOnaye*

solyanka (fish or meat soup) солянка *saLYANka*

someone кто-нибудь *KTO-nibut'*

something что-нибудь *SHTO-nibut'*

son сын *SYN*

soon скоро *SKOra*

sore throat ангина *anGIna*

soup суп *SUP*

sour cream сметана *smiTAna*

south юг *YUK*

souvenir сувенир *suviNIR*

Soviet совет *saVYET*

Soviet советский *saVYETski*

space космос *KOSmas*

spades (cards) пики *PIki*

spare part запчасть (*f*) *zapCHAST'*

spark plug свеча *sviCHA*

speak говорить (*i*) *gavaRIT'*, поговорить (*p*) *pagavaRIT'*

special особый *aSOby*

special delivery письмо с доставкой *piS'MO z daSTAFkay*

specialty (of the house) фирменное блюдо *FIRminaye BLYUda*

speed скорость (*f*) *SKOrast'*

spin кружиться (*i*) *kruZHYtsa*

spinach шпинат *shpiNAT*

splendid прекрасный *priKRASny*

sponge мочалка *maCHALka*

spoon ложка *LOSHka*

sporting goods спорттовары *sparttaVAry*

spot пятно *pitNO*

spring весна *viSNA;* **in the spring** весной *viSNOY*

square площадь (*f*) *PLOshat';* **Red Square** Красная площадь *KRASnaya PLOshat'*

stadium стадион *stadiON*

stage сцена *TSEna*

stainless steel нержавейка *nirzhaVYEYka*

stamp марка *MARka*

stand стоять (*i*) *staYAT'*

taxi stand стоянка такси *staYANka taKSI*

stand up вставать (*i*) *fstaVAT'*

starting time начало *naCHAla*

state (one of the United States) штат *SHTAT*

state государственный *gasuDARSTviny*

station станция *STANtsiya*

station (railroad) вокзал *vagZAL*

station-to-station на номер *na NOmir*

stationery канцелярский *kantsiLYARski*

steak бифштекс *bifSHTYEKS*

steal украсть (*p*) *uKRAST'*

steam room парильня *paRIL'nya*

steering wheel руль (*m*) *RUL',* рулевое колесо *ruliVOye kaliSO*

stem (of a watch) головка *gaLOFka*

stewed тушёный *tuSHOny*

stewed fruit компот *kamPOT*

stocking чулок *chuLOK*

stomach желудок *zhiLLUdak;* **upset stomach** желудочное расстройство *zhiLLUdachnaye raSTROYSTva*

stone камень (*f*) *KAmin'*

stop! стоп! *STOP*

stop (bus, trolley) остановка *astaNOFka*

stop (restrain) задержать (*p*) *zadirZHAT'*

stop (halt) остановиться (*p*) *astanaVItsa*

store магазин *magaZIN*

story (tale) рассказ *raSKAS*

straight прямой *priMOY;* **straight ahead** прямо *PRYAma*

strawberries клубника *klubNIka*

street улица *Ulitsa*

striking (extravagant) экстравагантное *ekstravaGANTnaye*

string шпагат *shpaGAT*

string beans ` стручковая фасоль *struchKOvaya faSOL'*

stripe полоска *paLOSka*

strong крепкий *KRYEPki*

student студент *stuDYENT*

stuffed cabbage голубцы *galupTSY*

sturgeon осетрина *asiTRIna*

sturgeon soup солянка *saLYANka*

stylish модный *MODny*

subway метро *miTRO*

such такой *taKOY*

suede замша *zamSHA*

sugar сахар *SAkhar*

suit костюм *kaSTYUM*

suitcase чемодан *chimaDAN*

summer лето *LYEta;* **in the summer** летом *LYEtam*

sun солнце *SONtse*

sunburn солнечный ожог *SOLnichny aZHOK*

Sunday воскресенье *vaskriSYEn'ye*

sunglasses солнечные очки *SOL nichniye achKI*

suntan загар *zaGAR*

suntan lotion крем от загара *KRYEM at zaGAra*

super: you're super! молодец! *malaDYETS*

supermarket гастроном *gastraNOM*

suppository свеча *sviCHA*

sweater свитер *SVItir*

sweet сладкий *SLATki*

swelling опухоль (*f*) *Opukhal'*

swim купаться(*i*) *kuPAtsa,* плавать (*i*) *PLAvat'*

swimming pool бассейн *baSYEYN*

switch выключатель (*m*) *vyklyuCHAtil'*

swollen вздут *VZDUT*

synagogue синагога *sinaGOga*

system система *siSTYEma*

T

table стол *STOL,* столик *STOlik*

tail light задняя фара *ZADniya FAra*

tailor ателье мод *atiL'YE MOT*

take, get взять (*p*) *VZYAT'*

take (escort) проводить (*i*) *pravaDIT'*

take (medicine) принимать (*i*) *priniMAT'*

take (transport by vehicle) отвезти (*p*) *atviSTI*

talcum тальк *TAL'K*

tall высокий *vySOki*

tampon тампон *tamPON*

tangerine мандарин *mandaRIN*

tape лента *LYENta,* плёнка *PLYONka*

TASS ТАСС *TAS*

tax налог *naLOK*

taxi такси (*n*) *taKSI*

taxi stand стоянка такси *staYANka taKSI*

tea чай *CHAY*

teacher преподаватель (*m*) *pripadaVAtil'*

telegram телеграмма *tiliGRAma*

telephone телефон *tiliFON*

telephone booth телефонная кабина *tiliFOnaya kaBIna;* **pay telephone** телефон-автомат *tiliFON-aftaMAT*

telephone call разговор *razgaVOR*

telephone receiver трубка *TRUPka*

television телевизор *tiliVIzar*

telex телекс *TYEliks*

temperature температура *timpiraTUra*

temporary временный *VRYEminy*

ten десять *DYEsit'*

tenth десятый *diSYAty*

terrible страшный *STRASHny*

terrycloth махровая ткань *maKHROvaya TKAN'*

thank you спасибо *spaSIba*

that one то *TO*

theater театр *tiATR*

their их *IKH*

there там *TAM*, туда *tuDA*

thermometer термометр *tirMOmitr*

they они *aNI*

thing вещь (*f*) *VYESH'*

think думать (*i*) *DUmat'*

third третий *TRYEti*

thirsty: I'm thirsty мне хочется пить *MNYE KHOchitsa PIT'*

thirteen тринадцать *triNAtsat'*

thirty тридцать *TRItsat'*

this это *'Eta*

thousand тысяча *TYsicha*

three три *TRI*

three hundred триста *TRISta*

threesome трое *TROye*

throat горло *GORla*

through через *CHEris*

thumbtack кнопка *KNOPka*

Thursday четверг *chitVYERK*

thus так *TAK*

ticket билет *biLYET*

ticket punch компостер *kamPOStir*

tie галстук *GALstuk*

tighten подвернуть (*p*) *padvirNUT'*

time время (*n*) *VRYEmya;* **how long (how much time)** сколько времени *SKOL'ka VRYEmini*

tint тон *TON*

tire шина *SHYna;* **the tire is flat** спустила шина *SPUStila SHYna*

tired (*m*) устал *uSTAL*

tired (*f*) устала *uSTAla*

tissue салфетка *salFYETka*

title название *naZVAniye*

to в *V*, на *NA*

toaster тостер *TOStir*

tobacco табак *taBAK*

today сегодня *siVODnya*

toenail ноготь (*m*) *NOgat'*

together вместе *VMYEStye*

toilet унитаз *uniTAS*

toilet paper туалетная бумажка *tualYETnaya buMAZHka*

toiletries shop парфюмерия *parfyuMYEriya*

tomato помидор *pamiDOR*

tomorrow завтра *ZAFtra*

tongue язык *yiZYK*

tonight сегодня вечером *siVODnya VYEchiram*

too (excessively) слишком *SLISHkam*

tooth зуб *ZUP*

toothache зубная боль *zubNAya BOL'*

toothbrush зубная щётка *zubNAya SHOTka*

toothpaste зубная паста *zubNAya PASta*

top: from the top сверху *SVYERkhu;* **on top** над *NAT*

topaz топаз *taPAS*

touch-up поправка *paPRAFka*

tourist турист *tuRIST*

tourist туристический *turiSTIchiski*

tourmaline турмалин *turmaLIN*

toward к *K*

towel полотенце *palaTYENtse*

tower башня *BASHnya*

toy игрушка *iGRUSHka*

trade торговля *tarGOvlya*

traffic движение *dviZHEniye*

train поезд *POyist*

train car вагон *vaGON*

tram/trolleycar трамвай *tramVAY*

transfer перевод *piriVOT*, переход *piriKHOT*

transfer передать (*p*) *piriDAT'*, пересесть (*p*) *piriSYEST'*

transformer трансформатор *transfarMAtar*

translation перевод *piriVOT*

transmission (auto) переключение скоростей *piriklyuCHEniye skaraSTYEY*

transportation перевозка *piriVOSka*, транспорт *TRANSpart*

traveler's check дорожный чек *daROZHny CHEK*

tree дерево *DYEriva*

trim подстричь (*p*) *padSTRICH'*

trip проезд *praYEST*

trolleybus троллейбус *traLYEYbus*

trout форель (*m*) *faRYEL'*

trunk (of a car) багажник *baGAZHnik*

try on примерить (*p*) *priMYErit'*

tsar царь (*m*) *TSAR'*

Tuesday вторник *FTORnik*

turkey индейка *inDYEYka*

turn (in a line) очередь (*f*) *Ochirit'*

turn оборот *abaROT*

turn повернуть (*p*) *pavirNUT'*

turnip репька *RYEP'ka*

turquoise бирюза *biRYUza*

tweezers щипчики *SHIPchiki*

twelve двенадцать *dviNAtsat'*

twenty двадцать *DVAtsat'*

twigs веник *VYEnik*

twisted растянут *raSTYAnut*

two два *DVA*

twosome двое *DVOye*

two hundred двести *DVYESti*

typewriter пишущая машина *PIshushaya maSHYna*

U

ugh! фу! *FU*

umbrella зонт *ZONT*

under под *POT*

underpants (men's) трусы *truSY*

undershirt майка *MAYka*

understand понимать (*i*) *paniMAT'*

undress раздеться (*p*) *razDYEtsa*

union союз *saYUS*

United States Соединённые Штаты *sayidiNYOniye SHTAty*

until до *DO*

until later! пока! *paKA*

up вверх *VVYERKH*

upset stomach желудочное расстройство *zhiLUdachnaye raSTROYSTva*

urgently срочно *SROCHna*

USA США *SA SHA A*

USSR СССР *ES ES ES ER*

U-turn разворот *razvaROT*

V

vacancy: no vacancy мест нет *MYEST NYET*

valley долина *daLIna*

valuable ценный *TSEny*

valuables ценные вещи *TSEniye VYEshi*

value (market) рыночная цена *RYnachnaya tsiNA*

van микроавтобус *mikraaFTObus*

vanilla сливочное *SLIvachnaye*

VCR видео-магнитофон *VIdio-magnitaFON*

veal телятина *tiLYAtina*

vegetables овощи *Ovashi*

velvet бархат *BARkhat*

velveteen вельвет *vil'VYET*

very очень *Ochin'*

(the) very самый *SAmy*

victory победа *paBYEda*

village село *siLO*

vinegar уксус *UKsus*

visa виза *VIza*

vitamin витамин *vitaMIN*

vodka вотка *VOTka*

vodka glass рюмка *RYUMka*

voice голос *GOlas*

voucher ваучер *VAUchir*

voyage: Bon voyage! Счастливого пути! *shastLIvava puTI*

W

waist талия *TAliya*

wait ждать (i) *ZHDAT'*, подождать (p) *padaZHDAT'*

waiter официант *afitsiANT*

waiter! молодой человек! *malaDOY chilaVYEK*

waitress официантка *afitsiANTka*

waitress! девушка! *DYEvushka*

wake разбудить (p) *razbuDIT'*

walk ходить (i) *khaDIT'*

wallet бумажник *buMAZHnik*

want хотеть (i) *khaTYET'*

I want	я хочу	*YA khaCHU*
you want	ты хочешь	*TY KHOchish*
he/she wants	он/она хочет	*ON/aNA KHOchit*
we want	мы хотим	*MY khaTIM*
you want	вы хотите	*VY khaTItye*
they want	они хотят	*aNI khaTYAT*

war война *vayNA*

warm тепло *tiPLO*

warm тёплый *TYOply*

wash, washing (of clothes) стирка *STIRka*

wash (clothes) стирать (i) *stiRAT'*

wash (shampoo) мытьё *myT'YO*

wash (give a shampoo) помыть голову *paMYT' GOlavu*

washbasin тазик *TAzik*

wash and wear немнущаяся ткань *niMNUshayasya TKAN'*

watch часы *chiSY*

water вода *vaDA*

watermelon арбуз *arBUS*

wave волна *valNA*

we мы *MY*

weak слабый *SLAby*

weakness слабость (f) *SLAbast'*

weather погода *paGOda*

wedding ring обручальное кольцо *abruCHAL'naye kal'TSO*

Wednesday среда *sriDA*

week неделя *niDYElya*

well! ну! *NU*

west запад *ZApat*

what что *SHTO*

wheel колесо *kaliSO*

when когда *kagDA*

where где *GDYE*

where from откуда *atKUda*

where to, which way куда *kuDA*

which какой *kaKOY,* который *kaTOry*

whipped взбитый *VZBIty*

whipped cream взбитые сливки *VZBItiye SLIFki*

white белый *BYEly*

who кто *KTO*

whose чей, чья, чьё, чьи *CHEY, CHYA, CHYO, CHI*

why почему *pachiMU*

wide широкий *shiROki*

wife жена *zhiNA*

will be быть (*i*) *BYT'*

I will be	я буду	*YA BUdu*
you will be	ты будешь	*TY BUdish*
he/she will be	он/она будет	*ON/aNA BUdit*
we will be	мы будем	*MY BUdim*
you will be	вы будете	*VY BUditye*
they will be	они будут	*aNI BUdut*

win выиграть (*p*) *VYigrat'*

wind ветер *VYEtir*

wind (a watch) заводить (*i*) *zavaDIT'*

window окно *akNO*

windshield ветровое стекло *vitraVOye stiKLO*

windshield wiper стеклочиститель (*m*) *stiklachiSTItil'*

wine вино *viNO*

winter зима *ziMA;* **in the winter** зимой *ziMOY*

wish желать (*i*) *zhiLAT'*

with с *S*

withdrawal slip расходный ордер *rasKHODny ORdir;* **make a withdrawal** принять вклад *priNYAT' FKLAT*

without без *BYES*

wolf волк *VOLK*

woman женщина *ZHENshina*

women's женский *ZHENski*

wonderful замечательно *zamiCHAtil'na*

wool шерсть (*f*) *SHERST'*

word слово *SLOva*

work работать (*i*) *raBOtat'*

worker, working рабочий *raBOchi*

worse хуже *KHUzhe*

would бы *BY*

wound рана *RAna*

wrap завернуть (*p*) *zavirNUT'*

wraparound накидка *naKITka*

wrench гаечный ключ *GAyichny KLYUCH*

wrist запястье *zaPYASt'ye*

wristwatch наручные часы *naRUCHniye chiSY*

write писать (*i*) *piSAT',* написать (*p*) *napiSAT';* **write down** записать (*p*) *zapiSAT';* **write out** выписать (*p*) *VYpisat'*

writer писатель *piSAtil'*

writing pad блокнот *blakNOT*

writing paper бумага для писем *buMAga dlya PIsim*

wrong: you've reached a wrong number вы не туда попали *VY NYE tuDA paPAli;* **something wrong** проблема *praBLYEma*

Y

yard ярд *YART*

year год *GOT*

yellow жёлтый *ZHOLty*

yes да *DA*

yesterday вчера *fchiRA*

yet уже *uZHE*

yield уступить (*p*) *ustuPIT'*

yogurt кефир *kiFIR*

you ты, вы *TY, VY*

young молодой *malaDOY*

young man! молодой человек! *malaDOY chilaVYEK*

your твой, твоя, твое, твои *TVOY, tvaYA, tvaYO, tvaI* ваш, ваша, ваше, ваши *VASH, VAsha, VAshe, VAshi*

Z

zero нуль (*m*) *NUL'*

zoo зоопарк *zaaPARK*

RUSSIAN—ENGLISH DICTIONARY

А

а and, but

абонементная книжка book of tickets

абрикос apricot

август August

авиаписьмо airmail letter

авоська "just in case" (string bag)

австралиец (*m*) Australian

австралийка (*f*) Australian

Австралия Australia

автобус bus

автодорожная карта road map

автоматически automatically

автоматический automatic

автомобиль (*m*) car

автор author

авторизованный authorized

автосервис auto repair shop

адаптер adapter

адвокат lawyer

администратор administrator

адрес address

Азия Asia

аквамарин aquamarine

аккумулятор car battery

аллергия allergy

амальгама amalgam filling

Америка America

американец (*m*) American

американка (*f*) American

американский American

аметист amethyst

амфитеатр rear orchestra

ананас pineapple

ангина sore throat

английский English

англичанин (*m*) British (Englishman)

англичанка (*f*) British (Englishwoman)

Англия England

антисептик antiseptic

антракт intermission

апельсин orange

апельсиновый orange

апрель (*m*) April

аптека pharmacy, drugstore

арбуз watermelon

аспирин aspirin

ассорти (*n*) assortment

ателье мод tailor

атлас satin

Африка Africa

ацетон nail polish remover

аэропорт airport

Б

багаж baggage

багажная бирка baggage claim check

багажник trunk (of a car)

баклажан eggplant

балет ballet

балкон balcony

балык filet of sturgeon

бампер bumper

банан banana
бандероль (*f*) printed matter
банк bank
банка can, jar
баня bathhouse
бар bar
баранина lamb
бархат velvet
бассейн swimming pool
батерейка, батерея battery
батон loaf
башня tower
беговые лыжи cross country
  skis
бедро hip
без without
безопасность (*f*) security
безрецептный nonprescription
белокурый blond
белый white
бельэтаж mezzanine
бензин gasoline
бензобак gas tank
бензоколонка service station
бензонасос fuel pump
Берёзка Beriozka Shop
бессоница insomnia
беф-строганов beef Stroganoff
библиотека library
бизнес business
бизнесмен businessman
билет ticket
бинокль (*m*) opera glasses
бинт bandage
бирка claim check
бирюза turquoise
бифштекс steak
бланк blank form
ближайший nearest
близко near
блинная pancake house
блокнот writing pad

блузка blouse
блюдо dish, food
бог god
Боже мой! My goodness!
бок side
более more
болезнь (*f*) sickness
болеть (*i*) ache; **болит** it
  hurts
болт bolt (fastener)
боль (*f*) pain, ache
больница hospital
больно painful, it hurts
больше more, larger
большой large
Большой театр Bolshoi
  Theater
борода beard
борщ beet soup
ботинки men's shoes
браслет bracelet
брат brother
брелок charm
бриллиант diamond
бритва razor
бритьё a shave
бровь (*f*) eyebrow
бронирование reservation
бронхит chest cold
брошь (*f*) brooch
брюки pants
брюнетка brunette
бубны diamonds (cards)
будильник alarm clock
будущий future; **в будущем
  году** next year
булавка pin
булочка roll
булочная bakery
бульон boullion
бумага paper
бумажник wallet
бумажный paper

бусы beads
бутерброд sandwich
бутылка bottle
буфет buffet, snack bar
бы would
бывать (*i*) to be
быстрый fast
быть (*i*) to be, will be
  я буду I will be
  ты будешь you will be
  он/она будет he/she will be
  мы будем we will be
  вы будете you will be
  они будут they will be
бюро bureau
бюро обслуживания service bureau
бюстгальтер bra

В

в in, into, to
вагон train car
валет jack (cards)
валюта foreign currency
варёный boiled
варенье jelly
варьете show
вата cotton
ваучер voucher
ваш, ваша, ваше, ваши your
вверх up
веер fan
век century
великий great (too big)
вельвет velveteen
веник bunch of twigs
вентилятор auto fan
вернуть(ся) (*p*) return
весна spring; **весной** in the spring
ветер wind
ветровое стекло windshield
ветчина ham

вечер evening; **вечером** in the evening
вешалка hanger
вещь (*f*) thing
взбитый whipped
взглянуть (*p*) look at
вздут swollen
взять (*p*) take, get
видео-магнитофон VCR
виза visa
вилка fork
вино wine
виноград grape(s)
виноградный grape
винтик screw
вискоза rayon
височка sideburn
витамин vitamin
вишня cherry
вклад deposit
вместе together
вне outside
вниз down
внутри inside
во время during
вовремя on time
вода water
водитель (*m*) driver
водительские права driver's license
водка vodka
возвращать(ся) (*i*) return
возраст age
войлок felt
война war
вокзал (railroad) station
вокруг around
волк wolf
волна wave
волос hair
восемнадцать eighteen
восемь eight

восемьдесят eighty

восемьсот eight hundred

воскресенье Sunday

восток east

востребование demand; **до востребования** general delivery

восьмой eighth

вот here is

врач doctor

временный temporary

время (*n*) time

сколько времени how long, how much time

все everyone

всё everything

вспышка flash

вставать (*i*) stand up

вставить (*p*) put in

вставной зуб false tooth

встреча meeting

встречный oncoming

вторник Tuesday

второй second

вход entrance

входить (*i*) enter; **входить в стоимость** included in the price

входной билет entrance ticket, cover charge

вчера yesterday

въезд entry

вы you (plural and polite singular)

вывыхнут dislocated

выдать вклад make a deposit

вызвать (*p*) call for, summon

выиграть (*p*) win

выйти (*p*) exit, get out

выключатель (*m*) switch

вылетать (*i*) fly away

выписать (*p*) write out

выпить (*p*) drink

высокий high, tall

выставка exhibition

выхлопная трубка exhaust pipe

выход exit

выходить (*i*) exit, get out

выходной день day off

Г

габардин gabardine

гаечный ключ wrench

газ butane gas

газета newspaper

газетный киоск newsstand

гайка nut

галерея gallery

галлон gallon

галстук tie

гардероб coatroom

гастроном supermarket

где where

гектар hectare

гигиенические салфетки sanitary napkins

главный main

гладить (*i*) press

глаз eye

гланц gloss

глажка ironing

глубоко deeply

говорить (*i*) speak

год year

годовщина anniversary

гол goal

голландский Dutch

голова head

головка stem of a watch

головной head; **головная боль** headache

голоден (*m*), **голодна** (*f*) hungry

голубой light blue

голубцы stuffed cabbage
горло throat
гора mountain
горные лыжи downhill skis
город city
горошек polka dot
горчица mustard
горчичник mustard plaster
горячий hot
господин Mister
госпожа Miss, Mrs.
ГОСТ ASA (film speed)
гостеприимство hospitality
гостиница hotel
государственный state
готово ready
градус degree (of temperature)
гражданин (*m*), **гражданка** (*f*) citizen
грамм gram
гранат pomegranate
грейпфрут grapefruit
гриб mushroom
гриль (*m*) grill
громко loudly
громче louder
грудь (*f*) breast
груша pear
губа lip
губка sponge
губная помада lipstick
гудок horn
гусь (*m*) goose

Д

да yes
далее farther
далеко far
дама queen (cards)
дать (*p*) give
дача dacha (country house)

два (*m*), **две** (*f*) two
двадцать twenty
двенадцать twelve
дверь (*f*) door
двести two hundred
движение traffic
двое twosome
дворец palace
Дворец съездов Palace of Congresses
двушка two-kopeck coin
девушка young girl, miss (to waitress)
девяносто ninety
девятнадцать nineteen
девятый ninth
девять nine
девятьсот nine hundred
дежурная "key lady"
дезодорант deodorant
действующий active
декабрь (*m*) December
декларация customs declaration
декларировать (*i*) declare
дело matter, business
денежный fiscal, money; **денежный перевод** money order
день (*m*) day; **днём** in the afternoon
деньги money
деревня countryside
деревья trees
десна gum
десятый tenth
десять ten
детектив mystery (film, novel)
дети children
детский children's
дешёвый cheap, inexpensive
джинсы jeans
диета diet

дипломат diplomat

директор director

дирижёр musical conductor

диск disc, disk

дискотека discotheque

длина length

длинный long

длиться (*i*) last

для for

до before, until

добрый good; **доброе утро** good morning; **добрый вечер** good evening; **добрый день** good afternoon

дождь (*m*) rain; **идёт дождь** it's raining

долго a long time

должен (*m*), **должна** (*f*) I must, I owe

долина valley

доллар dollar

дом home; **дома** at home; **домой** (to) home

домкрат auto jack

доплатно collect (telegram)

дорога road, path, way

дорогой dear, expensive

дорожка path

дорожный чек traveler's check

доска board

доставка delivery; **письмо с доставкой** special delivery letter

достижение achievement

достопримечательность (*f*) attraction

дочка daughter

дочь (*f*) daughter

друг friend

дуть (*i*) blow

думать (*i*) think

дурак fool

духи perfume

душ shower

дыня melon

дышать (*i*) breathe

дюйм inch

Е — Ё

Европа Europe

единый билет single ticket

ёлочка herringbone

ерунда nonsense

если if

есть (*i*) there is

ехать (*i*) go (by vehicle)

ещё another, more

жаль it's a pity; **как жаль** what a shame

жар fever

жареный fried

жаркий hot (temperature)

жать (*i*) pinch; **они жмут** they pinch

ждать (*i*) wait

жевать (*i*) chew

желать (*i*) wish

железнодорожный переезд railroad crossing

жёлтый yellow

желудок stomach

желудочное расстройство upset stomach

жемчуг pearl

жена wife

женат married (of a man)

женский ladies', women's

женский салон beauty parlor

женщина woman

живот abdomen

жульен   julienne
журнал   magazine

З

за   behind
заболеть (*p*)   fall ill
забронировать (*p*)   reserve
заведующий   manager
завернуть (*p*)   wrap
завивка   a permanent
заводить (*i*)   wind (a watch)
заводиться (*i*)   turn over (car)
завтра   tomorrow
завтрак   breakfast
загар   sunburn
задержать (*p*)   stop, restrain
задний   rear, tail
заехать (*p*)   pick up, drive by
зажигалка   lighter
зажигание   ignition
заказано   reserved
заказать (*p*)   order
заказное письмо   registered
   letter
заказывать (*i*)   order
заколка   bobby pin
закрывать(ся) (*i*)   close
закрыто   closed
закрыть(ся) (*p*)   close
закурить (*p*)   smoke
закуска   appetizer
закусочная   snack bar
зал   hall
залог   security deposit
заменить (*p*)   replace
замечательно   wonderful
замужем   married (of a woman)
замша   suede
занято   occupied

запад   west
запасный   emergency, spare
запасный выход   emergency
   exit
записать(ся) (*p*)   write down,
   register
запор   constipation
запрещено   prohibited
запчасть (*f*)   spare part
запястье   wrist
заранее   in advance
зарядить (*p*)   charge (the car
   battery)
затраты   expenses
заушник   eyeglass arm
зачёсывать (*i*)   comb
звать (*i*)   call;   **меня зовут**
   my name is;   **как вас зовут?**
   what is your name?
здание   building
здесь   here
здоровье   health;   **На**
   здоровье! Cheers! (to your
   health).
Здравствуйте! Hello!
зелёный   green
зеркало   mirror
зернистая икра   black caviar
зима   winter;   **зимой** in the
   winter
знать (*i*)   know
значить (*i*)   mean
значок   lapel pin
золото   gold
золотой   gold(en)
зонт   umbrella
зоопарк   zoo
зуб   tooth
зубной   dental
зубная боль   toothache
зубной врач   dentist
зубной протез   denture
зубной эликсир   mouthwash

И

и and
иголка needle
играть (*i*) play
игрушка toy
идти (*i*) go (by foot); **идите!** go!
из from
извинить (*p*) excuse; **извините!** excuse me!
издание edition
изделия goods
изумруд emerald
изюм raisin
икра caviar; **зернистая икра** black caviar; **кетовая икра** red caviar
или or
имущество property
имя (*n*) first name
инвалид handicapped
индейка turkey
иностранный foreign
инспекция inspection
институт institute
инструмент instrument
Интурист Intourist
инфекция infection
информация information
искусство art
история history
июль (*m*) July
июнь (*m*) June

Й

йод iodine

К

к toward
кабина cabin

каблук heel
кадр exposure (film)
каждый each, every
казаться (*i*) seem
как how
какой which
камень (*f*) stone
камера хранения checkroom
Канада Canada
канадец (*m*) Canadian
канадка (*f*) Canadian
канадский Canadian
канцелярский office, stationery
капля drop; **ушные капли** ear drops; **глазные капли** eye drops
капот hood
капуста cabbage
карандаш pencil
карат carat
карбюратор carburetor
карманный pocket
карп carp
карта card, map
картина picture
картофель (*m*) potatoes
касса cashier
кассета cassette
кататься (*i*) ride; **кататься на коньках** go ice skating; **кататься на лыжах** go skiing; **кататься на санках** go sledding
католический Catholic
кафе cafe
качество quality
каша warm cereal
кашель (*m*) cough
каштан chestnut
каштановый auburn
каюта cabin
кварта quart
кварцовый quartz

квас kvas

квашенная капуста sauerkraut

квитанция receipt

кекс cupcake, muffin

керамика ceramics

кефир yogurt-like beverage

кило, килограмм kilo(gram)

километр kilometer

киоск kiosk; **газетный киоск** newspaper stand

кипяток boiling water

кисть (*f*) hand

кладбище cemetery

класс class

классический classical

класть (*i*) put down; **не кладите трубку!** don't hang up!

клей glue

клетка plaid

клеющая лента Scotch tape

клубника strawberries

ключ key

книга book

книжный магазин book store

кнопка thumbtack

когда when

код города area code

кожа skin, leather

колбаса salami

колготки pantyhose

колено knee

колесо wheel, tire

коллега (*m & f*) colleague

коллекционный collector's

колода deck of cards

кольцо ring, circle

комбинация ladies' slip

комедия comedy

комиссионный магазин antique store

комитет committee

коммунистический communist

компактный диск CD (compact disc)

компостер ticket punch

компот stewed fruit

компьютерный computer

конверт envelope

кондитерская pastry shop

конец end

конечно of course

конкуренция competition

конституция constitution

контактная линза contact lens

контракт contract

контроль (*m*) control

конфета candy

концерт concert

кончать(ся) (*i*) end

коньки ice skates

коньяк cognac

кооперативный cooperative

кооператив cooperative

копейка kopeck

коридор corridor, lane

коричневый brown

кормить (*i*) feed, serve food

коробка box

королева queen

король (*m*) king

коронка dental crown

короткий short

корреспондент correspondent

космонавт cosmonaut

космос cosmos, space

костёл Catholic church

кость (*f*) bone

костюм suit

котлета cutlet

который who, what, which

кофе (*m*) coffee

краб crab

красивый beautiful

Красная площадь Red Square

красный red

кредитная карточка credit card

крем cream, lotion

Кремль (*m*) Kremlin

кремни flints

крепкий strong

крепления bindings

кровотечение bleeding

кровь (*f*) blood

кролик rabbit

кроме except

кружева lace

кружиться (*i*) spin; **голова кружится** I'm dizzy

крупа cold cereal

крупный large

кто who

кто-нибудь anyone

куда where to, which way

кудри curls

купальник bathing suit

купаться (*i*) swim

купе compartment

купить (*p*) buy

купюра bill (paper currency)

курить (*i*) smoke; **не курить** no smoking

курица chicken

курс course (currency exchange rate)

курящий smoking, smoker; **для курящих** smoking section

кусачки nail clippers

кусок piece, bar (of soap, etc)

кухня cuisine

Л

ладья rook (chess)

лак для волос hair spray

лампа lamp

лампочка bulb

лапша noodles

ластик eraser

левый left

лёгкий easy, light

лёгковой автомобиль passsenger car

лежать (*i*) lie (in bed)

лезвие razor blade

лекарство medicine; **рецептное лекарство** prescription medicine; **безрецептное лекарство** nonprescription medicine

Ленин Lenin

Ленинград Leningrad

лента tape, film

лес forest

лето summer; **летом** in the summer

лечь (*p*) lie down; **лечь в больницу** go to the hospital

ли if, whether

ликёр liqueur

лимон lemon

лимонад soft drink

линейка ruler; **бумага в линейку** lined paper

линза lens

линия line

лиса fox

литр liter

лифт elevator

лихорадка fever; **сенная лихорадка** hay fever

лицо face

личный personal

лишний extra

лодка boat

лодышка ankle

ложа box, loge

ложиться (*i*) lie down

ложка spoon
локоть (*m*) elbow
лосьон face lotion
лук onion
лучше better
лучший better
лыжи skis
любить (*i*) like, love
люкс deluxe

M

мавзолей mausoleum
магазин store, shop
магнезия magnesia
магнитофон cassette recorder
мазь (*f*) ointment
май May
майка undershirt
майонез mayonnaise
максимальный maximum
мал, мала, малы too small
малахит malachite
маленький little, small
малина raspberries
мало a little
мандарин tangerine
маникюр manicure
маникюрные ножницы cuticle scissors
марка stamp, brand
марлевый gauze; **марлевая салфетка** gauze (sanitary) napkin
март March
масло butter, oil
массаж massage
мат! checkmate!
матовый matte
матрац mattress
матрёшка nested doll

мать (*f*) mother
махорка chewing tobacco
махровая ткань terrycloth
машина car
медленный slow
медовуха mead
медсестра nurse
между between
междугородный intercity; **междугородный разговор** long-distance call
международный international
мелький small
менее less
ментол menthol
меньше less, smaller
меню (*n*) menu
место seat, place; **мест нет** no vacancies
месяц month
метр meter
метрдотель (*m*) maitre d'hotel
метро subway (metro)
мех fur
меховой fur
мечеть (*f*) mosque
микроавтобус van
микстура mixture; **микстура от кашля** cough syrup
милиционер cop
милиция police
миллиард billion
миллиметр millimeter
миллион million
миндаль (*m*) almonds
минеральная вода mineral water
минимальный minimal
минута minute; **минуточку!** just a minute!
младший younger, junior
много many, much

модный stylish, fashionable

может быть maybe, perhaps

можно may (one)

мой, моя, моё, мои mine

молодец! you're super!

молодой young

молодой человек! young man! waiter!

молоко milk

молоток hammer

молчать (*i*) shut up (silent)

монастырь (*m*) monastery

море sea

морковь (*f*) carrot

мороженое ice cream

морская болезнь sea sickness

Москва Moscow

мост bridge

мочалка sponge

мочь (*i*) can, be able to

я могу I can

ты можешь you can

он/она может he/she can

мы можем we can

вы можете you can

они могут they can

муж husband

мужской male, men's

мужчина man

музей museum

музыка music

музыкальный musical

мундштук cigarette holder

мы we

мыло soap

мытьё (*n*) wash (shampoo)

мэйк-ап make-up

мягкий soft

мясной meat

мясо meat

мяч ball

Н

на on, onto, to

набирать (*i*) dial

набор set, collection

набраться (*p*) accumulate

над on top of

надо must (one)

надувной inflatable, pneumatic

назад ago, backwards

название title

найти (*p*) find

накидка wraparound

налево to the left

наличные (деньги) cash

налог tax

написать (*p*) write

напиток beverage

направление direction

направо to the right

напротив opposite

народный folk, people's

наручные часы wristwatch

нарушение violation

нарыв abscess

насморк cold (in the head)

насос pump

наука science

научно-популярный science fiction

начало beginning, starting time

начинать(ся) (*i*) begin

наш, наша, наше, наши our

не no

неделя week

нейлон nylon

некурящий non-smoking; **для некурящих** non-smoking section

немного a little

немнущаяся ткань wash and wear

нержавейка stainless steel

несколько few

нет no

нефрит jade

нечего nothing

нижний lower; **нижняя юбка** half slip

никто no one

ничего nothing, never mind

но but

новый new

нога leg

ноготь (*m*) fingernail, toenail

нож knife

ножницы scissors

номер number, hotel room; **на номер** station-to-station call

норка mink

нормальный normal

нос nose

носильщик porter

носок sock

носовой платок handkerchief

ночной бар nightclub

ночь (*f*) night

ноябрь (*m*) November

нравиться like, be pleasing to

ну! well!

нужен, нужна, нужно, нужны necessary, I need

нуль (*m*) zero

О

о/об about

обвариться (*p*) burn oneself

обгон passing

обед lunch

обжаренный grilled

обменный курс exchange rate

обменять (*i*) exchange

оборот curve, turn

обратный return

обручальное кольцо engagement/wedding ring

обслуживаться (*i*) be waited on

обслуживание service

обувь (*f*) shoes

обхват circumference

объезд detour

объявляться (*i*) announce

обязательство obligation

овощи vegetables

овсянный oatmeal

овчина sheepskin

огонь (*m*) fire

ограничение restriction

огурец cucumber

одеваться (*i*) dress (oneself)

одежда clothing

одеколон cologne

одеяло blanket

один (*m*), **одна** (*f*) one

одиннадцать eleven

однотонный solid color

одолжить (*p*) lend

ожерелье necklace

ожог a burn

озеро lake

озноб chills

ой! ouch!

окно window

около near

октябрь (*m*) October

он he

она she

они they

оникс onyx

оно it

опаздывать (*i*) be late

опасность (*f*) caution

опасный dangerous

опера opera

оперетта operetta

оплата payment

оправа frame for eyeglasses

оптика optician

опухоль (*f*) swelling

орех nut

освобождённый exempt, free from

осень (*f*) fall; **осенью** in the fall

осетрина sturgeon

особый special

оставить (*p*) leave (something)

остановиться (*p*) stop (halt)

остановка (bus, trolley) stop, stopping

осторожно carefully

от from

отбивная котлета chop/cutlet

отвезти (*p*) take (by vehicle)

отвёртка screwdriver

отдел section

отдельно separately

отец father

открывать(ся) (*i*) open

открытка postcard

открыто open

открыть(ся) (*p*) open

откуда from where

отойти (*p*) go away

отплывать (*i*) sail away

отправка shipment

отправлять(ся) (*i*) leave, depart, send

отставать (*i*) lag behind; **они отстают** my watch is slow

отчество patronymic

офицер knight (chess)

официант waiter

официантка waitress

оценивать (*i*) appraise

очень very

очередь (*f*) turn in a line

очки eyeglasses

ошибиться (*p*) err

П

пакет box, packet

палец finger

палка pole

пальто coat

памятник monument

память (*f*) memory; **на память** in remembrance

пара pair

парикмахерская barber shop

парильня steam room

парк park

партер orchestra (in the theater)

партия (political) party

партнёр partner

парфюмерия toiletry shop

паспорт passport

пассажир passenger

паста paste

пастор minister (pastor)

пачка pack, package

пелёнка diaper

пельмени pelmeni, Siberian dumplings

пельменная pelmeni cafe

пеницилин penicillin

пепельница ashtray

первоначальный initial

первый first

перевод translation, transfer

переводчик interpreter

перевозка transportation

перегреваться (*i*) overheat

перед before, in front of

передать (*p*) transfer

переезд (vehicular) crossing

перезвонить (*p*) call back

переключение скоростей transmission; **автоматическое переключение скоростей** automatic transmission

перелом broken bone

перерыв break (recess)

пересесть (*p*) transfer

перетасовать (*p*) shuffle

переход transfer, (pedestrian) crossing

перец pepper

персик peach

перчатка glove

петь (*i*) sing

печёный baked

печень (*f*) liver

печенье cookie

пешеходный pedestrian

пешка pawn (chess)

пиво beer

пиджак jacket

пижама pajamas

пики spades (cards)

пилка nail file

пирог pie

пирожное pastry

писатель (*m*) writer

письмо letter

питательный nourishing, moisturizing

пить (*i*) drink; **мне хочется пить** I'm thirsty

пишущая машинка typewriter

плавать (*i*) swim

плавки bathing trunks

плакат poster

план map

планы plans

пластинка musical record

пластырь (*m*) adhesive tape

плата charge, fee, payment

платёж payment

платина platinum

платить (*i*) pay

платок kerchief; **носовой платок** handkerchief

платформа platform

платье dress

плащ raincoat

плёнка photographic film, tape

плечо shoulder

плиссированная ткань permanent press

пломба dental filling

плоскогубцы pliers

плохой bad, poor

площадь (*f*) square

пляж beach

по according to

победа victory

поближе nearer

поблизости near by

побольше more

побриться (*p*) have a shave

повернуть (*p*) turn

поворот curve, turn

повторить (*p*) repeat

повторять (*i*) repeat

поговорить (*p*) speak (with)

погода weather

под under

подарок gift

подвернуть (*p*) tighten

подешевле less expensive

подлиннее longer

подмётка sole of a shoe

подобный similar; **и тому подобное** and so forth

подождать (*p*) wait

подойти (*p*) approach

подороже more expensive

подравнять (*p*) even out

подстричь (*p*) trim

подтвердить (*p*) confirm

подушка pillow

поезд train

поехать (*p*) go (by vehicle); **поедем!** let's go!

пожалуйста please, you're welcome

пожар fire

Пожарная охрана Fire Department

поживать (*i*): **как вы поживаете?** how are you?

пожилой elderly

позавчера day before yesterday

позвать (*p*) call, summon

позвонить (*p*) call on the telephone

поздно late

позже later

познакомиться (*p*) get acquainted

позолоченый gold-plated

пойти (*p*) go (by foot)

пока! until later!

показать (*p*) show

покашлять (*p*) cough

покой peace (of mind)

покороче shorter

покупка purchase

пол floor

полдень (*m*) noon

поле field

полёт flight

поликлиника clinic

полиэфир polyester

полночь (*f*) midnight

половина half

положить (*p*) put, place

полоска stripe

полотенце towel

полотно linen

полусухое semi dry

получить (*p*) receive, pick up

помада: губная помада lipstick

помидор tomato

помочь (*p*) help; **помогите!** help!

помощь (*f*) help; **скорая помощь** first aid, ambulance

помыть (*p*) wash

понедельник Monday

понести (*p*) carry

понимать (*i*) understand

понос diarrhea

попасть (*p*) get to; **вы не туда попали** you've reached a wrong number

поплин poplin

поправка touch up

попробовать (*p*) sample

популярный popular

порез a cut

порезаться (*p*) cut oneself

портфель (*m*) briefcase

порядок order; **всё в порядке** everything is in order

посадка boarding, landing of an airplane

посадочный билет boarding pass

посветлее lighter

посидеть (*p*) sit

послать (*p*) send

после after

послезавтра day after tomorrow

посмотреть (*p*) look

посольство embassy

поставить (*p*) put in

поставка delivery

постричься (*p*) have a haircut

посчитать (*p*) count, add up

посылка package

потемнее darker

потерять (*p*) lose

почему why

починить (*p*) repair

почистить (*p*) clean

почта post office; **Главный Почтамт** General Post Office

почтовый postal

почтовый ящик mailbox

пошлина (customs) duty

пояс belt

правый right

право right, correct

православный Orthodox

праздник holiday

практически practically

прачечная laundry

прачечная самообслуживания laundromat

предпочитать (*i*) prefer

предприятие enterprise

представить(ся) (*p*) introduce (oneself)

преимущество advantage, right of way

прекрасный splendid

преподаватель (*m*) teacher

прибывать (*i*) arrive

прибыль (*f*) profit

привет! regards!

пригласить (*p*) invite

приёмная reception room, waiting room

прийти (*p*) arrive, come

примерить (*p*) try on

примерочная кабина changing room

принести (*p*) bring

принимать (*i*) accept, take (medicine)

приносить (*i*) bring

принято accepted, acceptable

принять вклад make a withdrawal

приплывать (*i*) land

приправа seasoning

прислоняться (*i*) lean on

пристань (*f*) dock

приступ attack; **сердечный приступ** heart attack

приходный ордер deposit slip

причёска hairdo

пришить (*p*) sew on

приятно pleasing

пробить (*p*) punch a ticket

проблема problem, something wrong

пробор part (in the hair)

проверить (*p*) check

проводить (*i*) take, escort

программка program

продавать (*i*) sell

продажа sale

проезд ride, trip

проездной билет trip ticket

проехать (*p*) get to

проиграть (*p*) lose a game

проигрыватель (*m*) record player

прокат rental; **на прокат** for rent

пропуск key card (pass)

просветить (*p*) X-ray

простить pardon; **простите!** pardon me!

простыня linen towel, sheet

протез (зубной) denture

протекать (*i*) leak

протестантский Protestant

профессия profession

прохладный cool

проход aisle

проходить (*i*) pass by

процесс process

прошлый past, previous; **в прошлом году** last year

прощайте! farewell!

проявлять (*i*) develop film

пруд pond

прямо straight ahead

прямой straight

птица bird

пуговица button
пудра powder
пункт point
пускать (*i*) let in
пусть let, allow
путеводитель (*m*) guidebook
путешествие trip
путь (*m*) way, path
пучок bun (hairdo)
пятнадцать fifteen
пятница Friday
пятно spot
пятый fifth
пять five
пятьдесят fifty
пятьсот five hundred

Р

работать (*i*) work
рабочий worker, working
раввин rabbi
рагу ragout
радиатор car radiator
радио radio
раз one time, once
разбить(ся) (*p*) break, shatter
разбудить (*p*) wake
разворот U-turn
разговор conversation, telephone call
разговорник phrasebook
раздеться (*p*) undress (oneself)
размен change (money)
разменять (*i*) change
размер size
разрешить (*p*) allow
разъединить (*p*) disconnect
рана wound
рано early
раскладушка cot

расписаться (*p*) sign
расписание schedule
рассказ short story
рассольник kidney soup
расстройство disorder; **желудочное расстройство** upset stomach
растение plant
растительное масло vegetable oil
растянут twisted
расходный ордер withdrawal slip
расходы expenses
расчёска comb
расчётный час check out time
ребро rib
революция revolution
регистрация registration, check in
редиска radish
резинка rubber band
резьба carved object
рейс flight
река river
рекомендовать (*i*) recommend
ремень (*m*) belt
ремень вентилятора (*m*) fan belt
ремонт repairs
репька turnip
ресница eyelash
республика republic
ресторан restaurant
рецепт prescription
рецептный отдел prescription section
решётка fender
ржаной rye
рис rice
рисование drawing
рождение birth; **с днём рождения!** happy birthday!

розетка plug
розничная цена retail price
розовый rose, pink
роман novel
российский Russian
Россия Russia
рост height
ростбиф roast beef
рот mouth
рубашка shirt
рубин ruby
рубль (*m*) ruble
рубчатый вельвет corduroy
рука arm
рукав sleeve
рукавица mitten
рулевое колесо steering wheel
руль (*m*) steering wheel
рулон roll (of something)
румяна rouge
русский (*m*) Russian, Russian man
русская (*f*) Russian woman
ручей brook
ручка pen, door handle
ручной hand
ручной тормоз hand brake
ручные часы wristwatch
рыба fish
рыбный fish
рынок market
рыночная цена market value (price)
рычаг lever; **рычаг переключения** gear shift
рюмка vodka glass
ряд row

C

с from, with
сад garden

салат salad, lettuce
салон section on a airplane
салфетка napkin, tissue
сам self
самолёт aircraft
самообслуживание self-service
самый the very (best, least)
сантиметр centimeter
санки sled
сапог boot
сапфир sapphire
сатин sateen
сауна sauna
сахар sugar
сахарин saccharin
сбить (*p*) knock over
сборник collection
свежий fresh
свёкла beets
сверху from the top
светить (*i*) shine
светлый light
свеча suppository, spark plug
свидание appointment; **до свидания** good-bye
свиной pork
свитер sweater
свободный free
священник priest
сдавать (*i*) deal the cards, give over
сделать (*p*) do, make
себе, себя oneself
север north
сегодня today
седьмой seventh
сейчас now
секунда second (sixtieth part of a minute)
секундная стрелка second hand
селёдка herring
село village
сёмга salmon

семнадцать seventeen

семь seven

семьдесят seventy

семьсот seven hundred

семья family

сенная лихорадка hay fever

сентябрь (*m*) September

сердце heart

серебро silver

серебряный silver

середина center

серый gray

серьга earring

серьёзно seriously

сестра sister

сзади in the back

сигарета cigarette

сигар cigar

сигнальный огонь directional signal

сидеть (*i*) sit

синагога synagogue

синий dark blue

система system

сказать (*p*) say

скользкий slippery

сколько how much, how many

скорая помощь first aid, ambulance

скоро soon

скорость (*f*) speed, gear

скотч Scotch tape

скрепка paper clip

слабительное laxative

слабость (*f*) weakness

слабый weak, mild

сладкий sweet

сладкое dessert

слайд slide

слева on the left

следующий next

слива plum

сливки cream

сливочное creamy (vanilla)

слишком too (excessively)

словарь (*m*) dictionary

слово word

сломать (*p*) break

слон bishop (chess)

слоновая кость ivory

служба service

случиться (*p*) happen

слушать (*i*) listen

слышно audible

смазать (*p*) grease

сменить (*p*) change, replace; **сменить масло** change the oil

смеситель (*m*) faucet

сметана sour cream

смородина currants

смотреть (*i*) look, see, watch

снег snow; **идёт снег** it's snowing

сниженный reduced; **товары по сниженным ценам** sale items

снимите! cut the deck!

снотворное sleeping pills

соболь (*m*) sable

собор cathedral

совет Soviet

советский Soviet

современный modern

совсем completely, entirely

Соединённые Штаты United States

сойти (*p*) go out; **вы с ума сошли?** are you crazy?

соковыжималка (*m*) blender

солнечные очки sun glasses

солнечный ожог sunburn

солнце sun

соль (*f*) salt

солянка solyanka (fish or meat soup)

сорок forty

сорочка shirt

сосиска hot dog

соуса sauce

социалистический socialist

союз union

спаржа asparagus

спасатель (*m*) lifeguard

спасибо thank you

спектакль (*m*) performance

спереди in the front

спешить (*i*) hurry; **они спешат** my watch is fast

спина back

спирт alcohol

список list

спичка match

спокойной ночи! good night!

спорттовары sporting goods

справа on the right

спрашивать (*i*) ask

спустить (*p*) descend; **спустила шина** the tire is flat

среда Wednesday

среди among

средний medium

срочно urgently

СССР USSR

стадион stadium

стакан glass

станция station

стартер starter

старший elder, senior

стекло glass, eyeglass lens

стеклочиститель (*m*) windshield wiper

стелька insole

стирать (*i*) wash clothes

стирка wash, washing (clothes)

стихотворение poetry

сто hundred

стоимость (*f*) cost, price

стоить (*i*) cost

стол desk, table

столик table

столовая cafeteria

стоп stop

сторона side

стоянка parking; **стоянка такси** taxi stand

стоять (*i*) stand; **стойте!** wait!

страна country

страница page

страхование insurance

страшный terrible

стрелка hand of a watch

стрижка haircut

стричь (*i*) cut hair

строитель (*m*) builder

стручковая фасоль string beans

студент student

ступня foot

суббота Saturday

сувенир souvenir

судак pike perch

судорога cramp

сумка pocketbook

сумма amount

суп soup

сурок marmot

сухой dry

сцена stage

сцепление gear shift, clutch pedal

счастливого пути! bon voyage!

счёт account, score

США USA

сын son

сыр cheese

сюда here

Т

табак tobacco

таблетка tablet

тазик washbasin
так so, thus, this way
такой such
также also
такси (*n*) taxi
талия waist
талон ticket, coupon
тальк talcum powder
там there
тампон tampon
танцевать (*i*) dance

тапочка slipper
тарелка plate
твой, твоя, твоё, твои your
творог cream cheese
театр theater
театральный theatrical
телевизор television
телеграмма telegram
тележка (baggage) cart
телекс telex
телефакс fax
телефон telephone
телефон-автомат pay telephone
телефонная кабина telephone booth
тело body
телятина veal
темно dark
тёмный dark
температура temperature
тень (*f*) shadow
тепло warm
тёплый warm
теплоход boat
термометр thermometer
тесны too narrow
тетрадь (*f*) notebook
тётя aunt
тише quieter
ткань (*f*) material, fabric
то that one

товарищ comrade
товары goods, items
только only
томатный tomato
тон tint
топаз topaz
торговля trade
торговый trade
тормоз brake
торт cake
тостер toaster
точилка sharpener
тошнота nausea
трагедия tragedy (drama)
трамвай tram, trolleycar
транспорт transportation
трансформатор transformer
треска cod
третий third
трефы clubs (cards)
три three
тридцать thirty
тринадцать thirteen
триста three hundred
трогать (*i*) touch; **не трогать** don't touch
трое threesome
троллейбус trolleybus
тропинка path
трубка pipe, telephone receiver
трубочный табак pipe tobacco
трусики ladies' panties
трусы men's underpants
туалет bathroom, restroom
туалетная бумажка toilet paper
туда there
туз ace (cards)
тупик dead end
турист tourist
туристический tourist; **туристический класс** economy class
турмалин tourmaline

туфли women's shoes
тушёный stewed
тушь (*f*) mascara
ты you (singular)
тыква pumpkin
тысяча thousand

утка duck
утро morning; **утром** in the morning
ухо ear
ушиб bruise
ушные капли ear drops

У

у at, near
убран cleaned, picked up
убыток a loss
увеличить (*p*) enlarge
удалить (*p*) pull (a tooth)
удлинитель (*m*) extension cord
удовольствие pleasure; **с удовольствием** with pleasure
уезжать (*i*) depart
ужасно awful
уже already
ужин dinner
укладка set (hairdo)
украсть (*p*) steal
украска color rinse
уксус vinegar
улыбаться (*i*) smile
ум mind
уметь (*i*) know how
умывальник sink
универмаг (универсальный магазин) department store
университет university
унитаз toilet
упасть (*p*) fall
уронить (*p*) drop
успокаивающее sedative
устал (*m*), **устала** (*f*) tired
уступить (*p*) yield
усы mustache

Ф

фамилия family name
фара headlight
фарфоровый porcelain
фасан pheasant
фасоль (*f*) beans
февраль (*m*) February
фен hair dryer
фига fig
фигура chess piece
фигурные коньки figure skates
фильм movie
фильтр filter
финик date (fruit)
фирма business firm
фирменное блюдо house specialty
фланель (*f*) flannel
фонарь (*m*) flashlight
фонд fund
форель (*m*) trout
фотоаппарат camera
фотографировать (*i*) photograph
фотография picture
фототовары photographic supplies
фрукты fruits
фу! ugh!
фунт pound
фут foot (measurement)
футбол soccer

Х

халат robe
хватить (*p*) be enough
хвост (pony) tail
химический chemical
химчистка dry cleaner's
хлеб bread
хлопчатобумажная ткань cotton fabric
ходить (*i*) go, walk
хозяйство economy
хозяйственный household
хоккей hockey
хоккейные коньки hockey skates
холодильник refrigerator
холодный cold
холм hill
хороший good
хорошо! that's good/okay!
хотеть(ся) (*i*) want, like
　я хочу I want
　ты хочешь you want
　он Хона хочет he/she wants
　мы хотим we want
　вы хотите you want
　они хотят they want
хрен horseradish
хрусталь (*m*) crystal
художественный artistic
художник artist
хуже worse

Ц

царь (*m*) tsar
цвет color
цветная капуста cauliflower
цветы flowers
цена price
ценный valuable
ценное письмо certified letter

центральный central
центр downtown
цепочка chain
церковь (*f*) church
цирк circus
цыплёнок chicken

Ч

чай tea
час hour, o'clock; **в котором часу?** at what time?
часовая стрелка hour hand
частичный partial
частник private taxi driver
часто often
часть (*f*) part
часы watch, clock
чей, чья, чьё, чьи whose
чек check, bill
чёлка bangs
человек person; **на человека** person-to-person call; **молодой человек!** young man! waiter!
чемодан suitcase
черви hearts (cards)
через across, through
чёрный black
чёрт devil; **чёрт возьми!** darn it!
чеснок garlic
четверг Thursday
четверо foursome
четвёртый fourth
четверть (*f*) quarter
четыре four
четыреста four hundred
четырнадцать fourteen
чинить (*i*) repair
число number, date; **какое сегодня число?** what's today's date?

чистка dry cleaning
читать (*i*) read
что what
что-нибудь something
чувствовать себя (*i*) feel
чулок stocking
чуть almost

Ш

шампанское champagne
шампунь (*m*) shampoo
шапка hat
шапочка cap
шарф scarf
шасси (*n*) chassis
шах! check! (in chess)
шахматы chess
шашечка check; в
   шашешку checked
шашки checkers
шашлык shish kebab
шашлычная shish kebab cafe
шведский стол smorgasbord
швейцар bellboy
шезлонг chaise longue
шёлк silk
шерсть (*f*) wool
шестнадцать sixteen
шестой sixth
шесть six
шестьдесят sixty
шестьсот six hundred
шея neck
шина car tire
широкий wide
шифон chiffon
шницель (*m*) Schnitzel
шнур cord
шнурок shoelace
шоколадный chocolate

шпагат string
шпилька bobby pin
шпинат spinach
штаны slacks
штат state
штука item
шуба fur coat

Щ

щека cheek
щёлочь (*f*) antacid
щётка brush
щи cabbage soup
щипчики tweezers

Ъ

ъ the hard sign

Ы

Ь

ь the soft sign

Э

экскурсионный excursion
экскурсия excursion
экскурсия по городу city tour
экстравагантный extravagant,
   striking
электрический electrical
электронный electronic
электронные часы digital
   watch
электротовары electrical
   supplies
эликсир; зубной эликсир
   mouthwash
Эрмитаж Hermitage

этаж   floor
это   this, that
эхо   echo

Ю

юбка   skirt
ювелирный   jewelry
юг   south
юмор   humor

Я

я   I
яблоко   apple

яблочный   apple
язык   tongue, language
яичница   omelet;
   яичница-болтунья
   scrambled eggs;
   яичница-глазунья   fried
   eggs
яйцо   egg; **яйцо вкрутую**
   hard-boiled egg; **яйцо
   всмятку**   soft-boiled egg
январь (*m*)   January
янтарь (*m*)   amber
ярд   yard (measurement)
ярус   (theater) circle, ring
яшма   jasper
ящик   box; **почтовый ящик**
   mailbox

INDEX

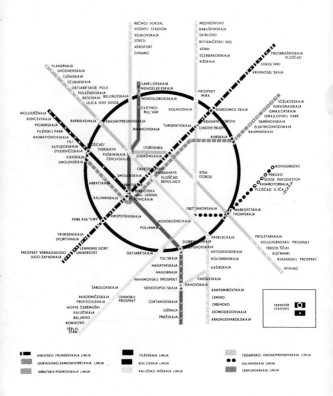

RECNOJ VOKZAL
VODNYJ STADION
VOJKOVSKAJA
SOKOL
AEROPORT
DINAMO

MEDVEDKOVO
BABUŠKINSKAJA
SVIBLOVO
BOTANIČESKIJ SAD
VDNH
ŠČERBAKOVSKAJA
RIŽSKAJA

PREOBRAŽENSKAJA
PLOŠČAD'
SOKOL'NIKI
KRASNOSEL'SKAJA

PLANERNAJA
SHODNENSKAJA
TUŠINSKAJA
ŠČUKINSKAJA
OKTJABR'SKOE POLE
POLEŽEVSKAJA
BEGOVAJA BELORUSSKAJA
ULICA 1905 GODA

SAVELOVSKAJA
MENDELEEVSKAJA

PROSPEKT
MIRA

ŠČELKOVSKAJA
PERVOMAJSKAJA
IZMAJLOVSKAJA
IZMAJLOVSKIJ PARK
SEMËNOVSKAJA
ELEKTROZAVODSKAJA
BAUMANSKAJA

MOLODEŽNAJA
KUNCEVSKAJA
PIONERSKAJA
FILËVSKIJ PARK
BAGRATIONOVSKAJA

BARRIKADNAJA KRASNOPRESNENSKAJA

CVETNOJ
BUL'VAR

KOLHOZNAJA

KOMSOMOL'SKAJA

MAJAKOVSKAJA

TURGEN'EVSKAJA

KRASNYE VOROTA
CHISTYE PRUDY

KURSKAJA

NOVOSLOBODSKAJA

FILI
KUTUZOVSKAJA
STUDENČESKAJA
KIEVSKAJA
SMOLENSKAJA

PLOŠČAD'
TVERSKAJA
PUŠKINSKAJA
ČEHOVSKAJA

LYUBJANKA

DZERŽINSKAJA

OKHOTNYJ RJAD
TEATRAL'NAJA
PLOŠČAD'
REVOLJUCII

KITAJ
GOROD

ARBATSKAJA

SMOLENSKAJA

NOVOGIREEVO
PEROVO
ŠOSSE ENTUZIASTOV
AVIAMOTORNAJA
PLOŠČAD' IL'IČA

KALININSKAJA

BIBLIOTEKA
imeni LENINA
BOROVICKAJA

PARK KUL'TURY

KROPOTKINSKAJA

NOVOKUZNECKAJA

TRET'JAKOVSKAJA

MARKSISTSKAJA
TAGANSKAJA

POLJANKA

FRUNZENSKAJA
SPORTIVNAJA

LENINSKIE GORY
UNIVERSITET

OKTJABR'SKAJA

DOBRYNINSKAJA
SERPUHOVSKAJA

PAVELECKAJA

PROLETARSKAJA
VOLGOGRADSKIJ PROSPEKT
TEKSTIL'ŠČIKI
KUZ'MINKI
RJAZANSKIJ PROSPEKT
VYHINO

PROSPEKT VERNADSKOGO
JUGO-ZAPADNAJA

AVTOZAVODSKAJA
KOLOMENSKAJA
KAŠIRSKAJA

TUL'SKAJA
NAGATINSKAJA
NAGORNAJA
NAHIMOVSKIJ PROSPEKT
SEVASTOPOL'SKAJA

VARŠAVSKAJA

KAHOVSKAJA

KANTEMIROVSKAJA
LENINO
OREHOVO
DOMODEDOVSKAJA
KRASNOGVARDEJSKAJA

ŠABOLOVSKAJA

AKADEMIČESKAJA
PROFSOJUZNAJA
NOVYE ČERËMUŠKI
KALUŽSKAJA
BELJAEVO
KON'KOVO
TËPLYJ
STAN

LENINSKIJ
PROSPEKT

ČERTANOVSKAJA

JUŽNAJA

PRAŽSKAJA

TRANSFER
STATIONS

KIROVSKO-FRUNZENSKAJA LINIJA

GOR'KOVSKO-ZAMOSKVORECKAJA LINIJA

ARBATSKO-POKROVSKAJA LINIJA

FILËVSKAJA LINIJA

KOL'CEVAJA LINIJA

KALUŽSKO-RIŽSKAJA LINIJA

TAGANSKO-KRASNOPRESNENSKAJA LINIJA

KALININSKAJA LINIJA

SERPUHOVSKAJA LINIJA